P9-EMR-075

"Regardless of your personal struggles, this book will provide real solutions. If you're a man with internal battles, this book will provide life-changing solutions. If you're a woman who wants to better understand her man's internal conflicts, this book offers powerful insights. With real-life examples Dr. Jantz keeps the reader engaged while making each point easy to comprehend and each solution simple to apply."

—**Timothy R. Jennings**, MD, FAPA, adjunct faculty,
University of Tennessee College of Medicine

"Men today face incredible challenges, and often they are reluctant to admit that anything is wrong and call in reinforcements. In *Battles Men Face*, Dr. Gregory Jantz helps men and the women who love them address these issues head-on. Each page offers insight and hope to build strength and bring personal victory."

—**Tim Clinton**, president, American Association
of Christian Counselors

Books by Gregory L. Jantz, PhD,
with Ann McMurray

Healing the Scars of Emotional Abuse
How to De-Stress Your Life
Every Woman's Guide to Managing Your Anger
Overcoming Anxiety, Worry, and Fear

BATTLES
MEN
FACE

STRATEGIES TO WIN THE WAR WITHIN

GREGORY L. JANTZ, PhD
WITH ANN MCMURRAY

a division of Baker Publishing Group
Grand Rapids, Michigan

© 2012 by Gregory L. Jantz

Published by Revell
a division of Baker Publishing Group
PO Box 6287, Grand Rapids, MI 49516-6287
www.revellbooks.com

Printed in the United States of America

All rights reserved. No part of this publication may be reproduced, stored in a retrieval system, or transmitted in any form or by any means—for example, electronic, photocopy, recording—without the prior written permission of the publisher. The only exception is brief quotations in printed reviews.

Library of Congress Cataloging-in-Publication Data
Jantz, Gregory L.
    Battles men face : strategies to win the war within / Gregory L. Jantz with Ann McMurray.
        p.   cm.
    Includes bibliographical references (p.   ).
    ISBN 978-0-8007-1969-2 (pbk.)
    1. Men—Religious life. 2. Christian life. I. McMurray, Ann. II. Title.
BV4528.2.J36 2012
248.8′42—dc23   2012022932

Unless otherwise indicated, Scripture quotations are from the Holy Bible, New International Version®. NIV®. Copyright © 1973, 1978, 1984, 2011 by Biblica, Inc.™ Used by permission of Zondervan. All rights reserved worldwide. www.zondervan.com.

Scripture quotations labeled MSG are from *The Message* by Eugene H. Peterson, copyright © 1993, 1994, 1995, 2000, 2001, 2002. Used by permission of NavPress Publishing Group. All rights reserved.

The internet addresses, email addresses, and phone numbers in this book are accurate at the time of publication. They are provided as a resource. Baker Publishing Group does not endorse them or vouch for their content or permanence.

The names of persons who have come to The Center for Counseling have been changed, and some illustrations are a combination of individual stories to protect confidentiality.

13   14   15   16   17   18   7   6   5   4   3   2

In keeping with biblical principles of creation stewardship, Baker Publishing Group advocates the responsible use of our natural resources. As a member of the Green Press Initiative, our company uses recycled paper when possible. The text paper of this book is composed in part of post-consumer waste.

This book is dedicated to all the men I've worked with over the years who had the courage to take that step of faith, walk into my office, and change their lives for good.

Contents

PART 3—THE HOW

Introduction

He was the president of a large regional company with multiple locations and almost a thousand employees. He owned two homes and a vacation bungalow on the coast. In his midfifties, he was fit and energetic, at least when I'd seen him in public at social functions. On this day, though, he was hunched over and deflated.

"I just don't get it," he admitted. "If I want something to happen in business, all I have to do is place a couple of calls and it's done. If I say 'go,' things move; if I say 'stop,' they do. I seem to have control over everything around me but me." His voice got very quiet. "And if I don't find a way to get myself under control, I could lose everything I value and worked so hard for."

I'll never forget that day—but not because what he said was so unique. I've heard the same thing, in one form or another, many times from people at a loss to understand why they can't control their slide toward disaster. I remember that day because it was a reminder that people who are powerful on the outside can still feel powerless on the inside, just like everyone else.

Another reason I remember this conversation is because it was a man talking. From the time I started counseling, most of my clients have been women. That's been slowly changing over the past several years, but even today the majority of people seen at my clinic are women. There seems to be a higher hurdle for men in our culture to admit they need help and to seek out counseling. It's even more remarkable to find a powerful man admitting he isn't able to fix things on his own. Here was a man firmly in charge of others but unable to control himself.

Men have a long history of being in charge of all sorts of things—except themselves. This lack of self-control in private can threaten to undo a lifetime of work and accomplishment in other, more public, arenas. Just like the executive that day, men can become frustrated and bewildered because what works to control the people in their lives fails to control their self.

Today, men continue to become enmeshed in compulsive behaviors that are destructive to their health, their work, and their sense of self, as well as to the ones they love. Sometimes it is the men who are fully in control of other aspects of their lives who find themselves trapped in secret compulsions. And sometimes it is these men who try and try to make progress toward change but end up sinking deeper and deeper into the compulsion for all that effort.

I get it. I'm a guy. I run my own business. I have people who work for me, and my job is to help other people figure out how to do what's right for them. I spend my life showing people how to take the necessary steps to change their lives for good. Yet, with all of that, I stumble myself. I know what to do, but I don't always do it. It's easy for me to take up the lament of the apostle Paul, who said in Romans 7:15, "I do not understand what I do. For what I want to do I do not do, but what I hate I do." Just like other men, I can easily find myself doing the very thing I hate.

So, while I am a counselor, I'm also a man who understands this strange world we inhabit, where we're told we're not in charge but often are expected to be; where taking action seems so natural but sometimes leads us down a very dark path; where we've been taught to elevate certain aspects of our personalities while burying others, only to find those buried parts continually trying to surface.

I'm also a Christian. I recognize that not everyone reading this book will be, and that's okay. I just want to be up front about who I am and where I'm coming from. If anything, this book is about men being honest, so it would be ridiculous, really, to try to cover up an essential part of who I am. I'm going to offer a lot of thoughts and examples and reasons in this book. You're not required to agree with every one. All I ask is that you give me a fair hearing.

As men, we really are in charge—at least of ourselves. We have free will. We may want to overlook our decisions or dismiss their consequences or blame others, but we are in charge, even when we're doing the very thing we hate. The difficulty is in knowing which part of us is in charge when we do the things we hate—where that part gets its power and how to take the power back. That's what this book is about. It's about how to stop doing the things you hate and take back control of your life and choices.

The WHAT

This book is set up in three sections to help you navigate the way to freedom from compulsive patterns. The first section is called "The WHAT" and will outline those behaviors particularly entangling to men.

Pornography

I said earlier that the ratio of women to men in my counseling practice has changed over the years, and one of the driving factors is the prevalence of pornography. This is a tremendously dangerous snare to many men. With the breadth of content available on the internet and the amoral reach of search engines, we live in an age uniquely designed for the lust of the eyes. Pornography is easily accessible, infinitely varied, and, for some men, incredibly compelling.

Sex

If pornography is the lust of the eyes, then sex could be said to be the lust of the heart. This is not sex as designed, an intimate merging of two people, but sex as an act of selfish fulfillment. When the act of sex becomes an addiction, it stops being the culmination of a relationship and becomes a physical act to be replicated over and over again, without regard to whom or why—it truly becomes just a what.

Anger

Whether slow to burn or quick to explode, anger is a powerful emotion. Banked with the white-hot coals of resentment, bitterness, and frustration, anger is the cause of much of the hurt men find themselves feeling and dispensing. Rage expelled in scalding outbursts provides a sense of release and empowerment. Left unchecked, however, it will eventually consume everything of value in a man's life.

Emotional Withdrawal

If anger is the spewing outward of toxic negativity, withdrawal is its inward counterpart, in which a person contracts emotionally into an island of self ever more isolated and fiercely defended. Thus protected, no one is able to get in; however, over time, you just may discover it harder and harder to find your way out.

Work

Each man has a finite amount of time on this earth, and a man, through his choices, determines where he will spend his time and with whom. Work is certainly able to give you a sense of purpose and accomplishment, but what happens when work becomes a curse? What happens when that sense of purpose you're looking for never seems to be fulfilled? What happens when that sense of accomplishment is always dangling just out of reach? There is no rest; there is no peace; there is no end to work.

Escape

Men have a role in family and society, regardless of the current cultural conversation. It is a role of responsibility, of protection and provision. When the rigors of this role and responsibility weigh too heavily, men can seek an escape route through taking on other roles. From weekend warriors to fantasy football, alternate realities that allow you to temporarily put aside your stresses and real-time concerns can be extremely compelling. You might find you're much happier escaping than you are living.

Deception

It's been said a man's word is his bond. However, some men seem incapable of not only telling the truth but also living the truth. In work dealings, they are dishonest, unreliable, and un-trustworthy, because what they say never actually ends up being what they do. These men leave a trail of frustrated friendships, truncated employments, broken promises, exasperated children, and fed-up spouses behind them. When you live your life saying one thing and doing another, all carefully clothed in excuses and rationales and reasons, you destabilize every relationship you have, including the one with yourself.

Competition

Competition is an empowering, motivational experience many of us grew up with. And it wasn't just the competition that was a blast, it was winning. We like to win. Experiencing a big win is a heady experience. When you're all about the win, when you'll wager just about anything for the thrill of risking it all, you just might be.

Consumption

Eating is pleasurable. Children are told what to eat and what not to eat, but adults make their own choices. Men often make their eating and drinking choices based on what they emotionally want rather than on what they physically need. Year after year, you can find your weight has increased and your health has decreased. You're not eighteen anymore, and it shows.

❧

The WHATs are going to hit the highlights of what I've seen entangle men over the years. I fully recognize, given the diversity of the human experience, I may have missed one or two. There is, however, a pattern to the WHATs, and that missing piece can easily be popped in and substituted for one of those I've outlined. Now isn't the time to get legalistic; now is the time to get help.

The WHYs

The next section of the book is called "The WHY." As a guy, you may be rolling your eyes, complaining that wanting to know *why* is the kind of thing you hear from your wife or girlfriend. Stay with me for just a bit and allow me to explain why understanding the WHY is so important. Say you were tasked with designing the wing of an airplane. You would certainly need to know what you were designing, but you would also need to know why it had to be designed that way. Why is a very important question. With airplane wings, why has to do with velocity and lift and drag. To design the wing correctly, you would need to know what it is supposed to do, but you'd also need to know why it reacts certain ways so you could be proactive in its design.

Aren't you at least as complex as the wing of an airplane? There are WHATs to your behavior and there are WHYs to your behavior. The WHATs can be easier to spot, but it is the WHYs that fuel the WHATs. If you don't tackle them both, you're not going to get to the core of the behavior. A job half done is a job undone; that's just the way it is.

Getting to know yourself better, to understand why you do what you do, is a valuable endeavor. Often, as men, we gain this sort of knowledge while doing something else—playing sports or climbing a mountain or rafting a river. The why we are the way we are can often seep into our understanding as a consequence of doing something else. There is great value in experiential learning. I would argue, however, that there is nothing wrong with an intentional, directed inner exploration, and in fact it can be quite valuable. This isn't meant as an endless journey without a destination but a targeted, plotted path to reach a specific goal of awareness so you can be better and stronger as a man. With awareness comes power to change. With awareness comes power to accomplish the personal tasks you set for yourself.

This doesn't have to be convoluted and complicated. Over the years, I've discovered there are just a few avenues to reaching the WHY.

Fear of Who You're Not

At the core of many compulsive behaviors is a deep-seated fear. Men who have often been told from infancy who they are supposed to be are afraid they do not measure up. This fear creates tension; tension cries out for release. Often the WHY of a compulsive behavior is a frantic attempt to numb and cover over fear of failure or inadequacy.

Fear of Who You Are

For some men, even more devastating than being found out for who you're not is being revealed for who you are. Often the WHY of a compulsive behavior is to shield and protect your inner man and all his faults. There is a terror of being discovered and rejected for who you are, so you use these compulsive behaviors to project out who you think you should be. But the bigger and more elaborate the mask, the more obvious it becomes, until the very behaviors meant to shield that inner self end up spotlighting its existence to those with eyes to see.

The HOW

As men, we're nothing if not practical. Show me what I'm doing; show me why I'm doing it; show me how to change, and I will. The final section of the book will go over the HOW, as in how to change.

Accept What Is

At the heart of true change is acceptance, though often it can seem the other way around. Restless, unsettled people change all the time, but it is not foundational, positive change. In order to find the strength to change, you need to know and accept who you are and who you're not. Acceptance allows you to live in reality and take real steps to change.

Love Yourself Enough to Say No

Some men think that becoming a man gives them the unlimited power to say yes. Reaching masculinity and reaching maturity, however, are two separate things. Maturity is found in your ability to say no even to yourself. In order for a man to find the strength and conviction to say no, he needs to develop a mature, tough self-love.

Live Face Forward

Life has a way of smacking us in the face. Sometimes life smacks us unfairly and sometimes life smacks us because we deserve it. Either way, each of us has a choice when we get smacked. We can stand there, stunned and immobile. We can retreat to our compulsion of choice as a way to ease the pain. Or we can move forward anyway. Standing still or retreating is a way of living backward. Change is found in forward gear.

Ask For and Accept Help

No man is an island, but most men still want to determine who comes on their particular plot of ground. It is important for you as a man to develop an accountability team, not a collection of yes-men or mindless buddies who will applaud or acquiesce to your compulsive behavior but mature men who will tell you to knock it off when necessary. For those of you who find yourself today without physical family, either through distance or estrangement or death, this group of guys can act as your band of brothers, with maybe even a father- or grandfather-type thrown in. Bringing others into your life and decisions doesn't mean giving away your personal power. Choose wisely and you'll actually increase it.

Getting a better handle on yourself and your life is worth it. Of course, you're only going to get out of this book what you put into it. I can give you information and insights, but I can't change you; that's not my job, that's yours.

To help you with that change process, at the end of each chapter there is a section called Taking Charge. This section gives you a way to think about what you've just read, to help anchor you with the main concepts and provide you an avenue for reflection and self-evaluation. Don't skip out on this part. In the famous words of that shoe company: Just Do It!

Finally, each chapter ends with a brief conclusion called Reaching Higher, and I guess you could call it the God part. Reaching Higher is my attempt to provide you with a short spiritual perspective on the themes of each chapter. I'm not a theologian, I'm a therapist, but I'm a therapist who infuses biblical principles and concepts into everything I do. It's who I am as a Christian, and it's only fair to give you all the components I believe are important to assist you in creating lasting, positive change in your life.

Thinking about what you're doing hasn't helped you change. Worrying about what you're doing hasn't been enough to make you stop. Hoping it would all just go away or wishing that people would just leave you alone so you wouldn't have to change hasn't really worked either. Bottom line: it's time to take this seriously and do something about it.

PART 1

THE WHAT

1

Pornography

The things that should disgust me don't anymore," he finally said. This was the second time I'd asked him to tell me what he was afraid of. The first time, he hadn't wanted to admit being afraid of anything and said fear wasn't the issue. The problem was he'd lost his job because he'd viewed pornography on his work computer, and his wife, who hadn't known about what he was doing at work, insisted he go for counseling. She'd really put her foot down after she'd yanked out the home computer and had a search done, finding just about everything he'd tried to erase over the past seven months. He was so humiliated by the blowup at work and his wife's reaction, he'd agreed to the counseling.

He'd agreed, but he really didn't want to be in an office with me, talking about this stuff. At first, getting anything out of him was like extracting tree sap in January. But when he finally did start to open up, all he wanted to talk about was how unfair they'd been at work and how it wasn't his fault and nobody had really been hurt and it was just a bunch of women in HR who had it in for him and if they'd just minded their own business things would still be okay with his wife. He'd been incensed that his wife hadn't trusted him and had spent money trying to trap him with the computer like he was some sort of criminal.

At that point, I'd stopped him and said this wasn't about any of them, it was about him and his addiction to pornography. He hadn't liked the word *addiction* either. He said it was just something he did to relax and take up time when he was bored. He said it was fun and no big deal. I reminded him his "no big deal" had resulted in the loss of his job and the potential loss of his marriage, so maybe that assessment wasn't entirely accurate.

He'd sat silent after that, and I just waited. In counseling there comes a moment of truth, if you will, when the person has to decide if they're going to work with you, if they're going to trust you or not. They have to decide if they're going to go with you, even when you veer off into areas they don't really want to go. If they don't want to go with you, they'll close down so fast, you can almost hear that mental door slam before they slam the physical door on their way out of your office. But, if they decide to trust, they leave the door open, sometimes just a crack, and allow you in. He decided to allow me in. Taking advantage of the invitation, I asked him again, "What are you afraid of?"

This time, he said he'd started out looking at what he considered to be "normal" pictures—of young women engaged in sexually provocative positions. He'd told himself it wasn't any worse than what he'd seen in *Playboy* as a kid and wasn't too far off from the latest Victoria Secret ad that had come in the mail. But once he started mining the internet for more of those types of pictures, he'd seen other types, and it wasn't long before he'd graduated from pictures of women-only to graphic depictions of sex acts, then from images to video, then from traditional to more unusual sex acts. Once he'd opened up that Pandora's box of pornography, with the virtually limitless quantity and content of the internet, the limits he'd set for himself began constantly shifting until, in his words, "the things that should disgust me don't anymore."

What he was appalled to admit was that not only did those things no longer disgust him, but they had actually begun to sexually stimulate him. That wasn't who he wanted to be but was terrified he had become. Now we had something to talk about.

Be Careful What You Wish For

There's a story in the Bible, in the Old Testament, about the people of Israel wandering in the desert after being freed by God from slavery in Egypt. In the story, because there's a whole lot of Israelites and not a lot to eat in the desert, God provides miracle food called manna. At first, it's the best thing, well, since sliced bread, and the Israelites love it. After a while, however, like everything, it seems, even manna gets old. The Bible says the Israelites cried out to God for meat because they were sick of the manna. They asked for meat and God provided—and then some. The Israelites ended up having meat not just one day but for a whole month until it came out of their "nostrils," and they ended up hating it (Num. 11:20). It's a classic—perhaps *the* classic—example of the old adage "Be careful what you wish for."

That's kind of what the internet has turned out to be in many ways, especially where pornography is concerned—a huge be-careful-what-you-wish-for. With the internet, you don't have to feel embarrassed going into the seedy corner market to buy one of those magazines kept behind the counter. You don't have to risk parking in front of an adult bookstore. You don't have to worry about being seen going into an X-rated film. Thanks to the internet, only you and your ISP ever need to know. Total freedom is a beautiful thing—with only yourself in charge and accountable. Of course, when it's just you in charge, that's when beautiful things can, sadly, turn ugly.

There is something to be said for accountability and fear of discovery. When you're contemplating doing something you know you really shouldn't, you have to weigh the risk of exposure. Generally, I've found that the more you don't want to be caught, the less likely it is something you should be doing in the first place.

This man got to the point where he was beating himself up over not only getting involved in pornography but also in allowing himself to entertain thoughts along such a deviant path. Over the course of our work together, I asked him why he hadn't just told his wife what he was doing or why he'd tried to remove evidence of what he was viewing from the computer. He said because he was ashamed but wanted to keep doing it. "At least," I reminded him, "you were ashamed. There was a part of you sounding a warning; you just chose not to listen." It would be hard, but he could choose to start listening.

In each of us, there is a voice that warns us when we're about to embark down a dangerous road. You can call it your conscience or the voice of experience or morality or sense of right and wrong. Whatever you want to call it, after we've become adults, it's about all we have going for us. There isn't a parent standing next to us anymore, warning us about the bus barreling down the street. Sure, there may be people around us, but they'll usually just stand by and watch as we get flattened by the 114 to downtown. No one is going to yank us out of the way; we've got to take that step ourselves. There's also no one to tell us to get up for work or eat our veggies or get to bed at a reasonable hour or look away from the computer screen. Those jobs have defaulted to us. Welcome to Adulthood. Welcome to Manhood.

Pornography's True Cost

One of those adult jobs for us as men is to stay away from pornography. It's difficult, however, because it's out there, everywhere, and—admit it—pornography can feel really good to view. If pornography didn't feel good, it wouldn't be such an issue. As men, we are wired to get a sexual charge out of a visual hit. And once that switch is flipped, it's hard to turn it off through sheer willpower. The mind may be screaming "Don't go there!" but the body is already running three steps ahead. In the headlong rush of sexual stimulation, it's easy to forget the true cost of continually saying yes to pornography.

Pornography Is Addictive

Of all the men I've counseled over the years on this issue, there have been only a handful who knew where they were headed when they started down the pornography road and, frankly, didn't care. The vast majority of men have been appalled to realize where their pornography addiction led them. They were so sure in the beginning that pornography would be only an occasional thing and they could stay firmly in control. As one "yes" turned into two and then more, each man developed reasonable-sounding rationales for his habit, as so many called it. After all, "habit" sounds much better than addiction. A habit is like biting your nails or drumming your fingers or humming under your breath. Habits can be annoying, sure, but ultimately they're harmless, right? Not this habit. Pornography does a great deal of harm, and not just to you.

Pornography, as a behavior, can be highly addictive and progressive. By progressive, I mean that what gave you a thrill to see or experience the first time wanes through repetition. In order to get the same sort of hit, you need to find something else, something new, something *more*. The internet is expert at providing something more because of the diversity of pornographic content available. There are no bumpers here, no rules to operate under; the internet is no-holds-barred. If you want *more*, you can have it in whatever type or genre or delivery method imaginable. You can keep going and going and going until what used to disgust you doesn't anymore. It may not even stimulate you anymore, and then you begin a search for the next thing. But the problem with the next thing is it's not really a thing. There's usually a person involved in there somewhere.

Pornography Objectifies People

There are all types of pornography, using a disturbing array of objects and/or behaviors to create sexual stimulation. Whatever the methodology, the delivery system is usually a person whose image is used as a visual hook. As such, this person—female, male, adult, young adult, adolescent, child, or even infant—loses their humanity and becomes merely a sexual object. This is called objectification, and it's one of the main arguments against pornography in the world today.

When you use another person to provide and gratify sexual stimulation, that person ceases to be a person, someone with a family—with a father who loves her just like you cherish your own children or with a brother who adores him like you do your own brother or with children who love her just like you do your own mother. When you objectify a person, you remove that person from their human context, including their family relationships. When you objectify a person in order to achieve your own sexual gratification, how can that do anything less than damage your own humanity—your own sense of compassion and connection to people as people?

Pornography Leads to Sexual Narcissism

Pornography creates a graphic fantasy. It portrays and provides a sexual experience that is not based on truth. It does, however, portray and provide a sexual experience that can be uniquely tailored to you as an individual. What would be impossible to coerce another person to do offline can be obtained online. You don't have to wait for what you want. You don't have to worry about a relationship or strings or responsibilities to get what you want. You don't have to be concerned about what the other person wants. You don't have to worry about real people knowing what you like to do. Pornography is ultimately all about you; it is sexual narcissism. As such, it sours real-life, offline relationships with people who have the right to tell you "no" or "not now" or "not that." Real people have their own preferences and needs. Real people get tired and put on weight and become ill. Real people have difficulty competing with airbrushed, polished images, false sentiments, and scripted responses. Pornography and the sexual narcissism it promotes is a relationship destroyer.

Pornography Corrupts the Mind

If a picture paints a thousand words, then pornography paints thousands of wrong words and images that will invariably intrude upon your mind when you least expect them or want them. I've worked with men who truly desired freedom from their pornography addiction, and all of them were haunted, even after they'd stopped, by the images they'd allowed themselves to view and the behaviors they'd allowed themselves to engage in. Part of the healing process was learning how to deal with all of those graphic afterimages seared into their brains. Their minds had been corrupted, and they often found themselves returning unwillingly to the very images they were trying so hard to exorcise.

Pornography Promotes Failure

If you say to yourself, "I'll never" or "That won't happen to me" or "I'm not like that" where pornography is concerned, you're already in danger. Pornography is powerful because it attaches itself to the human sex drive, which is immensely powerful. If you make yourself an exception to its power, you set yourself up for failure. If you believe you can stay in control and just look at this type of picture or say to yourself that opening one of those emails surely won't be a problem, you deceive yourself. Giving yourself excuses is leaving the door to your soul wide open and undefended. It is very unwise.

Pornography Undermines

As I said, the male sex drive is a powerful force—but it is quenchable. The ideal method of quenching and satisfying that drive is within a committed marriage relationship. The bonding of two people sexually is a divine gift and the glue of the relationship— the "one flesh" concept straight out of the Bible (Gen. 2:24). If you masturbate while viewing or engaging in pornography, you threaten to sexually starve your partner and create a division in your relationship. Pornography may start as an exciting view-only activity, but it rarely stays that way. Intentional sexual arousal usually demands eventual sexual release. Most men I've worked with conducted their pornography in secret and ended up masturbating in private. When you use yourself (no matter what type of pornography, you're still essentially using yourself) to satisfy your sexual desires, you make the other person in the relationship unnecessary. Unnecessary people can become unneeded and unwanted, marginalized and even despised. If you add personal guilt into this toxic mix, sometimes the only "use" for the other person is as someone to transfer your own guilt onto. The sex drive is powerful but so is the desire to blame someone else for our own choices—that's also in Genesis, if you'll remember the story of Adam and Eve. Then, not only do you starve the other person sexually, you use them as a scapegoat for your own feelings of despair and guilt. Released of a healthy sexual connection, you tie them instead to your blame and shame. Pornography does not enhance relationship; it mutilates it.

If you are single, pornography is not a suitable substitute for marital sex. Pornography is not a way for you to "handle" your sexual desires; it is not a safety valve that allows you to blow off sexual steam without engaging in physical sex. If you are a single man who is able to control your sexual desires and wish to remain single, great. But if you are a single man who finds yourself increasingly drawn to sexual release through pornography, you are going about such release down the wrong road. If you believe you can control the intensity and frequency of sexual desire through strategic use of pornography, you are again mistaken. Pornography does not quench sexual desire, pornography enflames sexual desire. God's gift of sexual fulfillment is given, ultimately, not through a physical act but through a relationship between a husband and wife.

Pornography Reflects a Dark Image

It is traumatic to work through a pornography addiction. It is traumatic because of the images viewed, the personal values torn to shreds, the relationships damaged, and the shocking realization that something you meant to control has actually taken control of you. It can be very traumatic to realize what you'll give up, what you'll exchange, and how far you're willing to go to continue in a sexually self-gratifying activity. When men finally come to their senses, they are often shocked at how far down into the cyber cesspool they've gone. Men who have always had self-confidence and assurance in their abilities and decisions are decimated by the knowledge of their willingness to give up everything of value for something they've come to consider so vile. It can be excruciating to see themselves as someone who will go back time and time again, as the Scriptures say, to eat their own vomit and bathe in their own filth (2 Peter 2:22). It is like seeing a reflection of self in a very dark mirror, a self-revelation of the worst kind.

Pornography promises to make you feel like more of a man and then works to strip away the values of manhood. It wrests control of your choices and decisions from you, rendering you impotent against it; it perverts how you view and appreciate women, corrupting your most intimate relationships; it exchanges the deeper satisfaction of living an honorable life for cheap, temporary thrills; it erodes your natural compassion and desire to protect women and instead exploits them for personal sexual satisfaction. Pornography warps who you are as a man. As such, pornography is your enemy, one out to destroy you.

Because of the work I do and the things I hear from others, I have to constantly keep my own mind and heart guarded. I do not consider myself above the temptations common to man because I have a doctorate or have written books. I am ever mindful of the admonition from the apostle Paul in Galatians 6:1: "Brothers and sisters, if someone is caught in a sin, you who live by the Spirit should restore that person gently. But watch yourselves, or you also may be tempted." For others and for myself, I truly believe that powerful things need to be carefully dealt with and closely monitored.

Rigged Game

Internet pornography is big business. There are literally millions of porn sites, with hundreds of millions of images generating worldwide billions of dollars.[1] These images constitute the worst impulses and deviant desires of mankind. The people involved in this business don't care about you; they don't care about the people used in the business; they care about the money. They are not interested in how a pornography addiction ruins your life; they care about how your pornography addiction enhances their bottom line.

In gambling, it's said you should never bet against the house, because the odds are in the house's favor. When it comes to pornography, the odds are in the industry's favor. They're banking on you saying yes just once to an image they push your way. They know if you say yes once, the odds are very good you'll say yes again and then maybe again. They're willing to put images out there for free to entice you to want more that you have to buy. You say yes even once at your own peril.

Strategic Retreat

In warfare, there are strategic initiatives and advances, but every battle should include plans for a strategic retreat. There are times when you're up against forces that are greater than yours. Fortunes shift in war, plans go awry, and you can find yourself in less-than-ideal conditions. Retreat need not necessarily signal surrender or defeat; sometimes it can lead to ultimate victory.

A poem credited to the Roman historian Tacitus says:

> He that fights and runs away,
> May turn and fight another day;
> But he that is in battle slain,
> Will never rise to fight again.[2]

Running away can seem cowardly. Yet we wage a constant battle against the lure of pornography, and we have to consider the advantages of a strategic retreat when presented with the opportunity to participate in pornography. The pornography business wants you slain, never to rise to fight the lure of their graphic images again. They want to own you, to take over your sense of control, and to dictate to you what you need to feel sexually fulfilled and satisfied. They want you dependent on them and the graphic images they provide to give you sexual gratification. They want to continue to use you to fund their exploitation of some other man's wife or daughter or son. Simply put, they want you enslaved by pornography, powerless and impotent; they want to exploit you, no less than they exploit those in the pornography itself.

A man who engages in pornography is not the picture of power but of capitulation. This is not the image of a strong, self-controlled man but a weak, co-opted one. This is not who men want to be, for themselves or for their families.

Do not deceive yourself into thinking that there is no harm done when you engage in pornography. There is tremendous harm being done. Your refusal to see it and your willingness to excuse it in no way reduce that harm; they only accentuate it. If you are involved in pornography, it's time to stop—right now.

Taking Charge

If I haven't convinced you through this chapter that pornography—for all the good you think it's providing in your life—is really a net negative, then I'm not sure what will. Do you need to read the United Nations reports on the exploitation of women and children from internet pornography or walk through some of the dark sewers of the international sex and pornography trade or interview someone the same age as your daughter or nephew or granddaughter who's been used and abused through pornography?

Enough with the excuses and the rationales and all the "buts" men use to justify their worst types of behavior. Part of being a man is having the courage to face up to the truth.

Be honest and ask yourself the following questions. Have the courage to be truthful. Courage needs to start somewhere, so why not here?

What type or types of pornography do you view?

How often do you view it?

Who knows about your use of pornography?

Do you usually masturbate while viewing pornography?

Have you told yourself you need to cut down on the frequency of your pornography use? If so, have you been able to do so?

Do you find yourself creating opportunities to be alone so you can engage in pornography?

Do you think about pornography on a regular basis, even when you're not engaged in it?

Has your use of pornography caused a problem with a past or current relationship? If so, was the difficulty resolved by you discontinuing your use of pornography? If not, was it resolved, and how?

Have you ever missed a social or family event specifically so you could engage in pornography undisturbed?

Have you ever thought that your life would be better if you hadn't started with all this pornography in the first place?

Have you told yourself you have to stop engaging in pornography? If so, have you been able to? If not, why not?

Finally, if you're open enough, I'll ask you the same question I asked the man at the start of this chapter: when it comes to your pornography use, what are you afraid of?

I realize for some of you, just going through this chapter has been unsettling and may have awakened a new or dormant desire for change. When it comes to something as powerful as pornography, change isn't always something you can tackle by yourself. If you have come to realize you need a partner, an ally, in this fight against pornography, I encourage you to seek out the help of a professional counselor or therapist. If you decide you'd like to work with a Christian counselor, I encourage you to go to the website of the American Association of Christian Counselors (www.aacc. net). I'm a member of AACC and know firsthand the integrity and value of that organization. Through their website, you can find Christian counselors in your area. You can also go to the website for my counseling practice, The Center, at www.aplaceofhope.com.

You don't have to tackle this on your own. The battle is yours to wage, but you can call on competent, professional reinforcements to give you the resources you need to claim victory over pornography.

Reaching Higher

Without fail, married men who are confronted with their pornography addiction will advance well-thought-out, logical reasons why they are, really, not at fault or not completely at fault. Single men will initially protest that the activity is harmless, though eventually admit they feel trapped, unable to stop. The truth is pornography is not harmless; it is a destructive, progressive addiction. The truth is that the responsibility for conquering it is yours and no one else's.

Making excuses and blaming others is age-old, but it doesn't impress God.

> Don't let anyone under pressure to give in to evil say, "God is trying to trip me up." God is impervious to evil, and puts evil in no one's

way. The temptation to give in to evil comes from us and only us. We have no one to blame but the leering, seducing flare-up of our own lust. Lust gets pregnant, and has a baby: sin! Sin grows up to adulthood, and becomes a real killer.

James 1:14–15 MSG

Pornography kills relationships. It kills true sexual intimacy and loots true masculinity. Pornography kills the decency and humanity of everyone involved in it. Don't settle; your sexuality was meant for more than that.

2

Sex

Before you start arguing with me that there's nothing wrong with having sex, and that, for you, it's *not* having sex that's the battle, allow me to elaborate on what I mean. In my practice, I work with men who are addicted to sex and who because of that addiction have come to hate it—hate what sex and their need for it does to them. It's like, once the sex drive gets turned on, their brains just go right out the window. What they want and value, the decisions and choices they make, get all messed up and twisted around until sex becomes not the one true pleasure in their lives but the one true nightmare.

"This woman was willing to give me sex. When we first got together, that's all that mattered to me." I'd asked him how this relationship that was causing so many problems in his life and with his family had gotten started. For something that wasn't overly complicated in the beginning, this relationship sure was ending up that way.

"Look," he said, "I've been divorced over four years, and, frankly, I wasn't getting much before we split up. When I started dating again, I found someone willing to give me sex. That's why we got together. I didn't think much beyond that." What had started out as a couple of evenings of sex a week had somehow turned into her staying overnight at his apartment. Within a couple of months, she had begun to move personal items into his spare bedroom, and then came the problem with her lease. Less than six months into the relationship, they were living together.

Because the sex continued, he didn't say much when her housing situation never seemed to get resolved. As one month became two and two became five, he found himself in a quandary. At first he hadn't asked her to pitch in on rent or help pay for the utilities because it was supposed to be temporary. Later, he was afraid if she started paying to live there, she would think it was a more permanent arrangement than he wanted. So, he said nothing and tried to cling to the "temporary" status quo.

The status quo hadn't lasted, at least with members of his family. His daughter wouldn't come over to his apartment because of the girlfriend, and the relationship was usually the subject of at least one argument when he and his daughter would meet at a restaurant for dinner. After almost a year, his daughter flatly refused to have anything to do with him as long as he was "still with that woman." In my office this man expressed genuine outrage over his daughter's reaction, incredulous that she thought she had any say whatsoever in whom he was with, just because that person wasn't her mother.

"Have you considered," I asked him, "that your daughter has no real cause for a relationship with her? After all, you chose this woman based primarily on sex. That's not a reason your twenty-three-year-old is going to share."

He told me he was torn. Part of him wished he could pull a lever and drop the relationship cleanly out of his life. He wasn't sure he'd ever had any real feelings for this woman; their relationship was centered in the bedroom not around the kitchen table. Now, even the sex had become unsatisfying and sporadic. He wanted her gone but was worried how he'd handle going back to "living like a monk," as he called it. Lately, it seemed whenever he felt the courage building to finally confront her about leaving, he'd find himself back in bed with her and at square one.

Signs of Sexual Addiction

There is something so fundamental about sex that it is difficult for people to view it as potentially addictive. Many men do not want to consider their patterns with sex as addictive because recovery from addictions often means abstinence from the substance or behavior, and sexual abstinence is not thought of as a viable, long-term option. It is only when the negative consequences of a sexual addiction continue to be present and to worsen that some men are willing to consider the possibility of addiction and search outside of self for answers and help.

Because I do so much work with eating disorders, it is easy for me to see the parallels between an eating disorder and a sexual addiction. Just like sex, eating was designed to be beneficial and positive, but it can become distorted. People were made to consume food, with the purpose to grow and nourish physical bodies and address physical needs. Those are eating's boundary markers, if you will. The problem develops when eating is moved out of those beneficial boundaries and is used to address other needs beyond physical nourishment. This is when eating becomes disordered, when it goes out of bounds and is used to meet emotional needs. Physical needs can be satiated; the body can become physically full. When food is used to fill emotional needs, there is no fullness; emotional needs can be cavernous, and no amount of controlling food or consuming food is enough.

So, what is a person to do if they have an eating disorder? Unlike alcoholics, who must abstain from alcohol to remain in recovery, the person with the eating disorder can't abstain from eating. In order to live, a person must continue to eat. The answer, then, for someone with an eating disorder is to discover where and how their eating went out of bounds, to intentionally unhook food and eating from the attempt to fill emotional needs, and to relearn healthy eating patterns. This places eating back within its proper boundaries and allows the person to recover.

In some ways, it is no different for a sexual addiction. Sex was created to be pleasurable and beneficial but was placed within boundaries. (As a Christian, I believe in the boundaries provided in Scripture, with sex as a beautiful and intimate act between a man and a woman within the setting of a committed marriage relationship.) When sex is moved out of those boundaries, it becomes disordered, just like eating. The answer is not always simply to abstain from sex. For many men, the answer is to discover where and how their sexual behaviors breached boundaries, to intentionally unhook sex from the attempt to fill distorted emotional needs, and to relearn healthy sexual behaviors.

In order to do the work to regain healthy sexual boundaries, a man must first understand and accept that the way he has been using sex in his life is unhealthy. This can be especially difficult when the sexual act itself produces such pleasure. In order to gain perspective, instead of concentrating on the act itself, you need to focus on the surrounding negative context of sexual addiction.

Preoccupation

We are sexual beings, yes, but we were not meant to be thinking about sex all the time. As men, we're wired to think about sex a great deal, but we're not animals—we're capable of control and context. A mind continually thinking about sex is an undisciplined mind. When your thoughts continually gravitate toward the sexual, this results in a perpetual state of sexual arousal.

Fantasizing

In order to maintain this arousal state, some men will begin to engage in sexualized fantasy, reliving actual sexual experiences or fantasizing about potential sexual experiences. Engaging in this fantasy life of anticipated sexual fulfillment can become more satisfying than the sexual act itself, which, when compared to a personalized, idealized fantasy, invariably comes up short.

Pornography

We've already talked about pornography, but it's important to recognize the role it plays in a sexual addiction. Engaging in pornography is a sexual act, whether or not it results in a physical release. Pornography is part of a disordered experience because it is grounded in sexual narcissism.

Sexualization

One of the negative consequences of sex removed from proper boundaries is the sexualization of other people and situations. When sex becomes the paramount experience in your life, then you begin to view all of your other experiences through a sexualized filter. People you come into contact with are immediately considered as possible sexual partners or potential objects of sexual fantasy. Nonsexual situations are colored with sexual hues either overtly, through sexual innuendo, joking, or comments, or covertly, through internal dialogue, thoughts, or fantasies. Sexualization occurs when every situation can result in a sexual joke, comment, or thought, when the very people you as a man were brought up to guard and protect become possible targets for gratification.

Continual Desire

When sex becomes the primary means by which you deal with uncomfortable or painful feelings such as anger, frustration, loneliness, boredom, invalidation, or lack of self-worth, your ability to deal with those feelings in other ways become atrophied. When sex is the one tool you reach for in order to feel better, to avoid feeling worse, or even to feel nothing at all, you chain yourself to a continual need for sex, not as a physical release but as an emotional one.

Time and Energy

Thinking about, planning for, engaging in, and recovering from sex requires time and energy. This is time and energy in competition with other areas of life. When sex is given supremacy, other areas of your life will, necessarily, suffer. Some men believe that sex is empowering and energizing, and it is, when held within its proper boundaries. Outside of those boundaries, sex can become a tyrant, bulldozing over other areas of life and responsibility, incessantly demanding and never fully satisfied.

Withdrawal from Activities and Relationships

As time and energy diminish because of the drain of a sexual addiction, you may find yourself reordering your priorities, saying no to so many good and valuable things in order to keep telling sex yes whenever and however it demands. You begin to withdraw from those people and things that are in the highest competition with sex. Your sexual addiction becomes a jealous, smothering lover.

Emotional Instability

The more sex is used as the answer to emotional needs, the more your emotional stability becomes tied to sex. Whether or not you have sex, whether or not that sex is what you wanted it to be, how you feel about yourself before, during, and after sex—all of that becomes the foundation for your emotional stability. Sexually addicted men I've worked with talk about their very sense of self becoming captive to that addiction. They come to hate themselves for their inability to gain control over their thoughts and actions, and this negative self-loathing ends up being spewed in rage inward toward self and outward toward those they love.

Inability to Cut Down or Stop

Counseling has not been Plan A for any of the men I've worked with. All of them first tried to get a handle on their sexual addiction themselves, to no avail. Each tried time periods of sexual restriction, lasting from a few days to mere hours, only to return to their behaviors with increased desperation. One of the telltale signs of sexual addiction is when you tell yourself on a regular basis you need to cut down or stop what you're doing yet find yourself failing over and over again.

Escalation of Behavior

Some people are able to stop, to restrict, through sheer will-power, but only for a time. An untreated addict will at some point inevitably break down in resolve and return even more strenuously to past behavior. This inability to stop can often partner with a desire for increased stimulation. You begin with pictures of one kind and graduate to graphics of a completely different sort. You begin with a single encounter and graduate to multiple encounters with multiple people. You begin with a single type of sexual partner and graduate to anyone who will give you sex. You begin with a certain type of sex and graduate to other methods, behaviors, and fetishes. An active addiction is never satisfied; it requires more and different to maintain the same level of gratification.

Failure to Heed Risks and Consequences

One of the most persuasive ways to help a man understand that sex has become an addiction is to show him the severe and negative consequences he has either experienced or risked in order to continue his sexual behaviors. This can be a sobering confrontation, depending on the severity of the behaviors and the depth of the consequences.

RELATIONSHIP CONSEQUENCES

A man with a sexual addiction may end up without any significant relationships. Addicts of any kind—sexual or otherwise—at some point become totally focused on the addiction. Spouses don't matter; children don't matter; parents don't matter; siblings don't matter; friends don't matter. The only thing that matters is the addiction. When the addiction is sex, the only thing that matters, then, is sex.

Other people in relationship with the sex addict become aware that something is hindering the relationship, even when they don't really know or understand what. Rarely will a sex addict initially confess to others about the truth of his addiction. Instead, in order to shield himself from shame and protect continuation of the sexual behaviors, the addict will maintain a high degree of secrecy. Part of the pattern of shielding includes blaming others for the consequences of the relationship breakdown produced by the hidden sexual behaviors. As blame is shifted to others, those relationships experience further deterioration.

When sex becomes more important than the person with whom you're having sex, it damages the relationship. At some point, the other person becomes aware that their sexual encounters with you are one-sided; it's really about you and fulfilling what you want. Healthy people don't appreciate being used like that. Healthy people will object and insist upon mutuality and respect within a sexual relationship. Healthy people will often leave or withdraw when respect and true intimacy are not given.

What repels healthy people in a sexual addiction can inversely attract unhealthy people. This creates a codependency, where your sexual addiction is then used by the other person to fill their own unhealthy needs. In this scenario, where each of you is feeding on the dysfunction of the other, there can be little external motivation for positive change within that relationship.

Most men do not start out openly jettisoning their other relationships. Instead, they develop a sort of double life, one that is lived in the "normal" world, and one that is lived in their sexualized self world. It is almost as if they split themselves in two, with each part living their respective lives, keeping as much separation between the two as possible. I've known a pastor who kept up this double life of pornography and prostitution until an affair with a parishioner brought that secret life to light. I've known a successful businessman, lauded in the community for his outward devotion to family, shattered when this inward double life was exposed through an errant email. The media reports on a regular basis about men whose double life is exposed, to the devastation of career, family, and professional standing.

Double lives are artificial constructs meant to avoid consequences and maintain the addiction as long as possible. I've seen men maintain these double lives for months and years. But the longer they go on, the more cracks appear in the carefully constructed façade. Lies have a way of working to the surface. Loved ones develop sensitivity to deception and either expend their own energies to uncover the truth or jettison the relationship altogether as too much work. Healthy people, still committed to remaining in the relationship, hover at its edges—on edge—maintaining a relational escape route as a personal survival strategy. When healthy people flee because of the pressures of this double life, unhealthy people can crowd in to fill the gap.

FINANCIAL CONSEQUENCES

There are usually direct financial consequences to a sexual addiction. These can range from the cost of purchasing pornographic material to paying for prostitutes. It can involve monetary gifts to keep a person close and payoffs to keep them away. It can include anything from the cost of representation in legal difficulties brought on by sexual activities to paying for a divorce lawyer. Depending on the type of activities engaged in to satisfy a sexual addiction, the financial consequences can also involve doctors and medical intervention. In addition, once a man decides to get help, his recovery from sexual addiction may require financial resources, depending on treatment options and insurance coverage.

EMPLOYMENT CONSEQUENCES

Some of the men I've worked with over the years have described how their work has suffered due to their sexual addiction. I've known men who lost their jobs due to viewing pornography. I've known men who lost their positions because of sexual encounters in the workplace. I've known men who left lucrative positions in order to start over in a new job or a new city when rumors of their double life began to percolate. I've known men who specifically took less engaging, lower-rung jobs in order to have the time, energy, and anonymity necessary to engage in their primary passion—their sexual addiction.

Earlier I said that a sexual addiction requires time and energy. There are two areas from which this time and energy are drained—one is from a man's relationships and the other is from a man's work. Sex becomes The Relationship and sex becomes The Work. Employers are willing to pay you to produce results professionally; they have little patience and zero tolerance for you engaging in any type of sexual activity in the workplace. With sexual harassment laws and the risk of potential litigation, even otherwise valued employees find themselves summarily dismissed. The good old boy network of overlooking or even encouraging sexual activity at work no longer exists, nor should it.

Health Consequences

A sexual addiction comes with health consequences. Unprotected sexual encounters can lead to a long list of sexually transmitted diseases. When you hook up with a prostitute, you place yourself in physical danger, and not only from the prostitute. No, masturbation does not lead to blindness, but it is possible to masturbate to the extreme and cause physical damage.

When an addict is in the throes of their addiction, physical consequences are considered temporary setbacks, not permanent roadblocks. Even serious, life-threatening conditions such as AIDS have sadly not proven enough motivation for some men to change, and thus sexually transmitted diseases continue to spread.

However, the severer the health consequences, the greater the wake-up call. Even more than relationship consequences or financial consequences or employment consequences, health consequences have the power to get a man's attention. In the heady spin of a sexual addiction, a man can feel aloof from the real world, in a cocoon of invincibility. All of that can come crashing down when his health and life are threatened by his actions. When a man is able to recognize the life-threatening nature of his behaviors and extrapolate that threat onto other areas of importance in his life, he is able to find a motivation strong enough to drown out the siren song of his sexual addiction.

Taking Charge

I recognize that many of you reading over this chapter have not encountered the severity of sexual addiction described here. Perhaps you've seen it in others you've known or experienced it through a family member or close friend. You're breathing that proverbial sigh of relief and saying, "That is not me." Really? You couldn't identify with even one of those signs? You didn't feel, not even once, that jolt in the pit of your stomach? Wasn't there anything that caught your attention and made you question if there isn't something more to what you're doing than you thought? Perhaps not, but even if the signs of a sexual addiction don't fit you, it is important for you to know what they are, to be aware of the signs so you can guard yourself against stepping too close to that edge.

For those of you who read through this material and felt yourself skimming over the surface of most of these signs, maybe resonating with one or two and only marginally, I urge you to continue to work through this section. I'm going to ask you to be honest about the role sex has in your life—past, present, and future—and develop some core sexual principles you want to hold on to as you continue through life.

Your Sexual Past

At what age do you remember becoming aware of yourself as a sexual person?

What was your first encounter with a sexual activity, including masturbation?

In your family, how was sex dealt with? Was it talked about?

Did you ever receive "the sex talk" from a parent or family member?

Do you remember your reaction to "the sex talk" and, if so, what was it?

What were some of the falsehoods you heard about sex?

Did you believe them and, if so, when did you stop believing them?

Is there anything you're ashamed of doing or feeling sexually as a child? As a teenager?

Were you ever approached sexually as a child by an adult or another child?

How do you believe that encounter affected you at that time?

At what age did you become sexually active?

Do you regret that sexual activity?

If you could erase a sexual incident from your past, what would it be and why?

Your Sexual Present

What is the nature of your sexual activity in the present? Are you abstinent, sporadic, active?

Are you satisfied with the choices you are currently making sexually?

How have your past sexual experiences affected the way you approach sex today?

Consider the ways you gain sexual satisfaction currently (including any of the patterns listed in this chapter). Do these activities reflect your values, principles, and aspirations?

Do any of your sexual behaviors cause hurt to yourself or another person? If so, be specific as to who and how.

Are you willing to express your remorse and ask for forgiveness from anyone you've hurt?

Are you willing to find a way to forgive yourself for the pain you've caused in your own life?

What would it mean to you to be forgiven for the pain you've caused because of your sexual behaviors?

Describe what is good and healthy about how you approach sex today.

Your Sexual Future

Thinking about your past sexual legacy and your present sexual reality, what would you like to see for yourself sexually? Name three sexual goals for the future:

1. _____

2. _____

3. _____

In order to achieve these goals, what would you need to retain in your life and what would you need to remove? Name three things for each:

Things to Retain

1. _____

2. _____

3. _____

Things to Remove

1. _____

2. _____

3. _____

You are a sexual being and are responsible for how you live out your sexuality. You are accountable to yourself and you are accountable to others for how you use sex within your life. If you identified with three or more characteristics outlined in this chapter, I strongly urge you to immediately seek out help. A trained counselor can assist you in determining whether or not you have a sexual addiction and, if so, how to begin a strategic plan of treatment and recovery. It is, simply put, a miserable existence to be in the clutches of a sexual addiction. Contrary to popular belief, it is not a life filled with satisfaction and fulfillment; it is a life filled with self-loathing, desperation, pain, and despair. You don't have to live that way any longer. There is no shame in admitting you need help and seeking it. There is no defeat in admitting you cannot tackle your behaviors on your own. Find the strength to say, "I need help," and then go out and get it.

Reaching Higher

The Bible is not timid when it comes to discussing sex. God is aware that sex is powerful and compelling; that's exactly how he created it. As with so many of the pleasures God designed in this life, he gave us sex and expects us to use it wisely. He also warns us of the consequences of using sex unwisely. Here is one example from Proverbs 7 (MSG):

Dear friend, do what I tell you; treasure my careful
　　instructions.
Do what I say and you'll live well.
　　　My teaching is as precious as your eyesight—guard it!
Write it out on the back of your hands;
　　etch it on the chambers of your heart.
Talk to Wisdom as to a sister.
　　　Treat Insight as your companion.
They'll be with you to fend off the Temptress—
　　that smooth-talking, honey-tongued Seductress.

As I stood at the window of my house
　　looking out through the shutters,
Watching the mindless crowd stroll by,
　　　I spotted a young man without any sense
Arriving at the corner of the street where she lived,
　　then turning up the path to her house.
It was dusk, the evening coming on,
　　the darkness thickening into night.
Just then, a woman met him—
　　she'd been lying in wait for him, dressed to seduce him.
Brazen and brash she was,
　　restless and roaming, never at home,
Walking the streets, loitering in the mall,
　　hanging out at every corner in town.

She threw her arms around him and kissed him,
　　boldly took his arm and said,
"I've got all the makings for a feast—
　　today I made my offerings, my vows are all paid,
So now I've come to find you,
　　hoping to catch sight of your face—and here you are!
I've spread fresh, clean sheets on my bed,
　　colorful imported linens.

My bed is aromatic with spices
  and exotic fragrances.
Come, let's make love all night,
  spend the night in ecstatic lovemaking!
My husband's not home; he's away on business,
  and he won't be back for a month."

Soon she has him eating out of her hand,
  bewitched by her honeyed speech.
Before you know it, he's trotting behind her,
  like a calf led to the butcher shop,
Like a stag lured into ambush
  and then shot with an arrow,
Like a bird flying into a net
  not knowing that its flying life is over.

So, friends, listen to me,
  take these words of mine most seriously.
Don't fool around with a woman like that;
  don't even stroll through her neighborhood.
Countless victims come under her spell;
  she's the death of many a poor man.
She runs a halfway house to hell,
  fits you out with a shroud and a coffin.

The shroud and the coffin part, the trotting behind her like a calf to the butcher shop part, is what turns the dream of sex into a nightmare for men who use sex unwisely. Solomon's wisdom has been out there, available through Scripture, for thousands of years. What is it going to take to get you to start listening?

3

Anger

Randy liked being angry; he liked the way it felt. Anger allowed Randy to see things clearly in his mind. When he was angry, he couldn't be talked into doing something he didn't want to do or be compelled to act a certain way if that wasn't him. Anger was like an impenetrable shield. He felt strong when he was angry. He felt energized. He liked it so much, he'd made sure his anger was never far away; Randy could call it up on a moment's notice.

Before Randy found anger, his primary response to life had been fear. Fear of being left alone by a mother who placed him close to the bottom of her daily priority list. Randy was expected to go along with whatever she was doing and not make trouble or to stay at home alone and not make trouble. He was auxiliary to his mother's life; at least, that's how it felt. Early on, he figured out where he stood with her and was terrified one day she'd just move on without him and not look back.

Randy grew up wanting to be noticed by his mother, but he dreaded being noticed by his father. His father was not a very nice person; Randy had heard that whispered by teachers over the years and out loud by some of his friends. He couldn't really argue; it was true. Randy's father drank quite a bit when he was home, and he tended to have only two settings—one, ignore everything going on around him, or two, yell at everything going on around him, including Randy, his mother, and his siblings.

In Randy's house, anger was presented strictly as an adult prerogative. Randy was not permitted to be angry, and that suited him at the time. With his father, showing anger made you visible, a target. With his mother, showing anger meant you were punished, left alone. Randy rarely got angry with his siblings, all younger than him, because he and his siblings tended to operate as a pack, trying to make it through each day essentially unharmed. Anger wasn't worth it, so Randy kept himself from feeling it.

That was when he was younger. There was a point in time, however, when Randy uncorked that bottle. In fifth grade, he found himself furious at another boy in school. Twenty-two years later, and it was still as fresh in his mind as if it happened yesterday. Near the end of that school year, kids were restless with summer mere days away, so the two fifth-grade teachers decided to combine classes and let the kids stay out longer at recess to run out their energy.

A group of the boys decided to play baseball. When Randy got up, he hit the ball and ran to first. He beat the tag because the boy playing first base dropped the ball. Instead of admitting it, the boy quickly scooped the ball back into his hand and made it look like the tag was good. The teachers were over by the monkey bars talking, too far away to see anything. Because it happened so fast, no one believed Randy.

Normally, Randy wouldn't have said anything, but for some reason, this time was different. He got mad; he was incensed that the boy had lied and that nobody believed him. He was mad at the teachers for not being there to see what happened. He was so mad, all of a sudden he didn't care what the boy thought or what the other kids thought or what the teachers thought.

The anger he felt burned away his fear. Randy felt cleansed. It was an amazing feeling. Instead of being scared or worried, he felt strong. At ten, he still wasn't strong enough to try this newfound discovery at home, but school was different, and it was different that summer with kids in the neighborhood.

When Randy was fourteen, he took his anger home. His mother quickly gave up on him, with mumbled comments about how he was growing up "just like" his father. Randy's mother never got angry; that was too much effort. Instead, she just found a way to fade into the background. Compared to his mother's apathetic withdrawal, his father's anger was impressive. But that anger, so intimidating to a six-year-old, even to a ten-year-old, wasn't nearly as impressive against his fourteen-year-old teenage anger.

When Randy brought his own anger home, he soon realized how weak his father's anger actually was. It was all yelling and cussing, but there was nothing solid behind it. His father's anger was perfunctory, just a way to get what he wanted, which was to be left alone to watch television, to read the paper, to listen to the news, to drink. The anger didn't seem to give his father any real strength. Instead, his father's anger made him winded and sweaty—he couldn't seem to keep it up for long. Compared to Randy's fourteen-year-old anger, his father's middle-aged anger was toothless and pathetic.

As soon as he was eighteen and done with high school, Randy was expected to either move out or pay rent. He knew he wasn't going to spend a dime to stay one more day in that house, so he moved out, taking his anger with him. When he moved from apartment to apartment, from job to job, from city to city, his anger always went along. Over the years, he learned to control it a bit, not let it out too much in the wrong situation, like when he was dating his wife, but it never left him completely. Randy made sure to keep his anger in reserve because he'd always found it useful.

That is, until the day, as a father, he found himself yelling in anger at a terrified three-year-old. Until the day Randy realized he'd not only become *a* father, he'd become *his* father. That's the day fear began to claw its way up over the top of the anger and back into the forefront of Randy's life. Now Randy was angry, but he was also afraid. The only way to truly get rid of the fear was for Randy to learn how to put his anger to better use.

Rooting Out Anger

I realize that's a fairly drawn-out story, but I told it that way for a reason: anger may seem like a short-fused emotion, but it can come with very long roots. I've heard Randy's story repeated over and over, just with differing details. The core of the story always remains the same—the destructive power of anger in the lives of men.

Anger produces a rush of adrenaline; it creates a physical response. Men get angry for all the reasons Randy did: to feel strong, to feel energized, to feel focused. Anger can be used as a shield, but we would be less than honest if we did not also admit that anger can be used as a weapon. Men who started out using anger as a shield, generally when they were children, often find that the temptation to lash out and use that anger as a weapon becomes irresistible as they get older. When you combine the adrenal and emotional punch of anger with male physicality, the potential for very real harm is multiplied. While it is true that men will lash out and hurt total strangers, I believe the bulk of the damage done by men's anger is directed toward those they care about the most.

There is an old song by Allan Roberts and Doris Fisher called "You Always Hurt the One You Love." I don't really know when it was written, but it had to have been a while ago. Wikipedia says it was performed by the Mills Brothers in 1944, by Ringo Starr in 1970, and by Ryan Gosling in 2010. That's quite a shelf life. Its longevity may have something to do with the lyrics by Doris Fisher, which acknowledge the sad truth that those nearest to you are the ones who get hurt the most. Its time-tested lament of hurting those you love is so true when it comes to men and their anger.

I don't believe most men want to use the anger they have built up inside to hurt those they love. Men are very tied to their loved ones, yet they are also tied to their anger and have difficulty letting it go. They tend to rationalize their anger, to explain it away, to blame it on others. This, also, is time-tested. In the twisted world of rationalized anger, the harsh word that breaks a heart, as the song says, masquerades as proof of true love. Our capacity for denial and excuse is often as large as our capacity for anger.

Because of that capacity for denial and excuse, it is important for men to understand the forms anger takes. We're all familiar with famous personalities whose angry outbursts resulted in trashed hotel rooms, confrontations with paparazzi, and threatened lawsuits. Certainly, that is one form of anger, but there are others beyond a raging bull.

The Slow Burn

Some men who have been brought up under circumstances where anger was not permitted, release their anger not as a white-hot flash but a continual slow burn. These men keep the fires of anger banked and fueled but low. They will often release this anger in less overt ways, through a cutting comment, a disparaging opinion, sarcastic and caustic humor, or railing against circumstances instead of people. They twitch; they murmur; they sigh. If you ask a slow burn man if he's angry, he will often deny it. Instead, he'll attempt to shake off the charge of anger and put it back on you, as a form of misunderstanding. When pressed, he may admit to being frustrated or irritated but never angry.

On the outside, he denies his anger, but on the inside, his internal dialogue with himself makes sure to stoke the fire. He will often feel marginalized, mistreated, as if life and its situations are against him. This perpetual state of low-level anger can result in physical symptoms of stress, such as digestive problems, headaches, and high blood pressure.

The Flash Burn

While the slow burn man attempts to conceal his anger, the flash burn man doesn't care. If he's angry, he doesn't care who knows it. People call him short-fused or hot-tempered. He gets angry quickly, strongly, but doesn't stay angry for long. He uses the brevity of his anger to justify its intensity. Once his anger has faded, he's ready to "move on" and can find it difficult to understand why other people continue to react to his anger after he's finished with it. Because he's "done" with his anger so quickly, he often fails to track how often or how strongly it flares up.

The Smoldering Coals

Unlike the slow burn man, the smoldering coals man is not as acutely aware of his anger. This man thinks he's put out the fire of his anger, has moved on or isn't affected by his anger any longer. This is a form of denial, so it can be extremely unsettling when his anger flares to life because of smoldering coals of anger he's left unattended.

I read a news story about two young men who were arrested in Arizona for causing the worst wildfire in that state's history.[3] These cousins left their campfire to go hiking. According to the story, they thought the fire was out when they left because they threw a candy wrapper on it and the wrapper didn't burn. At least, the wrapper didn't burn before they left. It burned after, though, and took 538,000 acres of eastern Arizona with it.

That's the danger of smoldering coals. They can appear to be out, but any stray piece of brush—an innocent circumstance, a misinterpreted comment, an unexpected difficulty—can cause that anger to rage back to life. Because those feelings have been left unattended, unbanked, the anger can easily overrun boundaries and quickly explode out of control, leaving behind the relational equivalent of scorched earth.

Outbreaks of Anger

Anger comes with a strong voice; anger is verbal. Sometimes that voice comes across loud and clear, broadcast at high decibels. Sometimes that voice is quiet, a rigidly controlled voice of rage, whose whispered threats are far more frightening than a yelled outburst. Sometimes that voice is kept contained within unspoken thoughts, silent to others but deafening to the man himself. The voice of anger often makes use of inherited dialogue, as if a script for anger has been passed down from one generation to the next.

Verbal anger is not confined to a bellow or a shout.

- Anger can also show itself as a pattern of sarcasm, cynicism, or criticism.
- Anger can show itself through overpoliteness, with precise pronunciation substituting for physical blows.
- Anger can show itself as a flat, monotone speaking voice, announcing its very presence by the lack of emotion.

- Anger can show itself as frustration or having a high IQ—Irritability Quotient.
- Anger can show itself as an immediate and defensive response.
- Anger can show itself by insisting it always has the last word in any conversation or conflict.
- Anger can show itself through manipulating through guilt, through playing the "shame and blame" game.
- Anger can show itself by issuing orders instead of asking for opinions.
- Anger can show itself by talking negatively of others.

The voice of anger can become so familiar, so intimate, it can be difficult to recognize as such. It becomes "just the way I am" or "just the way I talk." The more prevalent the voice of anger, the more comfortable with it you become. The danger, of course, lies when the voice of anger becomes indistinguishable from your own voice.

Anger comes with an emotional context—anger is emotional. Some men consider anger to be a physical response, not an emotional one, because they would never consider themselves "emotional" when they are angry. These men feel that anger is a way to deflect emotions; they become angry so they don't feel hurt or pain or shame or guilt. They do not see anger itself as an immensely powerful emotional response to life. Instead of admitting to feeling anger, men will say they are "keyed up" or "agitated" or "blowing off steam," considering the anger reaction as just part of being a guy.

At the root of anger is an array of negative feelings many men have been taught they should not feel—bewilderment, shame, guilt, indecisiveness, vulnerability. So, men can become angry when they sense these feelings welling up because they "know" they shouldn't have them. Anger tries to cover them up as they escape into rage.

Anger comes with a physical component; anger is muscular. Anger isn't just how you feel; it is also how you act. Physical expression of anger comes in a variety of forms, not always the classic backhanded blow.

- Anger can show itself as procrastination, the intentional slowing down of movements or tasks as a way to show displeasure.
- Anger can show itself as always being late.
- Anger can show itself as saying one thing but doing another.
- Anger can show itself as frequent sighing, huffing, or exhalations of air.
- Anger can show itself as frequent smiling, as if anger holds a special secret it's unwilling to share.
- Anger can show itself as difficulty falling or staying asleep.
- Anger can show itself in fatigue or apathy.
- Anger can show itself as clenched teeth, fists, or muscles.
- Anger can show itself as digestive problems and stomach ulcers.

The body knows when you're angry, even when you don't admit it to yourself. Anger produces an adrenaline (also called epinephrine, which is a powerful hormone and neurotransmitter) surge. This surge is known as the fight-or-flight response, which triggers specific physical results such as increased blood pressure, rapid heart rate and breathing, tunnel vision, increased nutrient release—all of these things get your body "ready" for either fight or flight. This fight-or-flight reaction is spontaneous and autonomic. You know when you're experiencing it because of the way you feel.

However, if you're someone who was taught or decided it was wrong to be angry, you may interpret these physical signs as something else. You may say you're keyed up or stressed out or out of sorts or frustrated. You may be very adept at convincing yourself you're not angry—but pay attention to your body. It will reveal what's really happening and when that anger fight-or-flight response has been triggered. Saying to yourself that you're not an angry person just because you've never hit anyone is not a comprehensive enough filter.

Men need to be aware of what I call "stealth anger," which can also be called passive-aggressive behavior. A passive-aggressive person appears to be compliant (passive) but is actually defiant (aggressive). A great description of passive-aggressive behavior came from a friend of mine who likened it to a dog who licks your face while it pees on your leg. The passive-aggressive man complies on the outside to what is being asked of him, but on the inside he rebels and finds a way to negate compliance through action. He may agree to go to the in-laws for dinner on Saturday but find a way to be called in to work instead, claiming he has no choice but to comply. He may tell his wife he'll mow the lawn but will work on his car until it's too late to mow, blaming a defective part or the complexity of the job. He may sign off on performance reviews about being to work on time but continue to arrive late, citing traffic, accidents, or unforeseen problems at home. The passive-aggressive man finds a way to do what he wants while trying to maintain the appearance he's acting the way he should.

This hiding of the truth can become a highly engaging game for some men. Touting their good intentions, they minimize the consequences of their actions. In doing so, these men tend to blame other people, circumstances, situations, unforeseen forces for the disconnect between what they say and what they do. They play the role of the victim while retaining ultimate control of their actions.

Anger is a powerful persuader. Anger can manipulate how you feel about yourself, your situation in life, how you interact with others. Anger can remove doubt, confusion, or indecision. Anger can make you feel invincible, righteous, vindicated, entitled. Each of these feelings places you in a position of power. Power is heady; it feels good.

While anger feels good to you, it may not feel good to others. Anger can be frightening, especially to people who are subordinate to you or physically weaker than you. It may get you what you want, but it does not produce the results you're really looking for. Most men do not want those around them to respond out of a sense of fear or intimidation. Instead, they really are looking for validation, acceptance, and love. However, those men who are convinced they are unworthy of any of those things will often settle for anger and the fear it brings if that's the only way they think they can get what they need. Anger is a handy, versatile tool, but it so easily damages those it's used on.

Using Anger Poorly

Men have been shortchanged over the past several years by a culture that tells them it isn't appropriate to get angry or express anger. There are only a few acceptable venues for anger expression—sports and military service. Unless you become a soldier or a member of the NFL, you are kind of out of luck on the venting anger front. I can understand where part of this comes from—the inappropriate and abusive use of anger by men in the past. But asking men to deny such a fundamental physical and emotional response has had its negative consequences. Instead of being trained how to effectively and appropriately deal with their anger, men in recent years have been told not to have any anger at all. That's unrealistic.

As I've worked with men, I've noticed different ways that they cope with this anger that they aren't allowed to acknowledge or express:

- *Obsessive sports*. Since sports is one of the venues for "acceptable" anger and aggression, it can become a place of expression and refuge for anger.

- *Sexual addiction*. The pursuit and conquest aspects of sex can become an outlet for the charged-up, adrenaline-saturated angry male.

- *Substance abuse and addictions*. What do you do when you're so angry you don't know what to do? Some men attempt to remove that overwhelming rage by making it go away, for just a little while. Alcohol and drugs can become a strategy to numb the pain and rage. At the core of many addictive behaviors is a desire to numb overwhelming feelings of repressed anger.

- *Power and control*. Some men choose an opposite path and give full vent to their anger and rage by manipulating and controlling those around them through threats of violence and actual violence.

- *Spiritual abuse*. Anger is one thing, but *righteous* anger is another. Some men find the Bible or other religious texts to be the perfect bludgeon to use on other people as a way to channel their anger and rage.

- *Depression*. After years of fighting against an ever-present sense of rage, some men capitulate into a state of despair and apathy, concluding it's better to feel nothing at all instead of anger all the time.

- *Financial issues*. Money is powerful, just like anger, so it's not surprising these two can find common inroads into a man's life and decisions. Money and financial success can be seen as vindication, as a way to compensate, for feelings of anger. This desire to fuel anger into the acquisition of money and power can lead a man into dangerous, foolish financial decisions based on jealousy and greed.

• *Isolation.* Some men retreat into a solitary place where they can be alone with their anger. (We'll talk more about this in the next chapter.)

Anger, then, is a true two-edged sword. My suggestion to men is to learn to use their anger in constructive ways instead of destructive ways. The only way to really learn to use anger—instead of anger using you—is to know where your anger comes from. And the only way to know where your anger comes from is to allow yourself to relive those significant moments of pain—physical pain and emotional pain. You have to understand your anger in order to harness it, just like a wild horse, to use it to motivate you to act in noble, beneficial ways. Misunderstood, undirected anger can be used to injure others; understood, harnessed anger can be used to protect others. One of the hallmarks of being a man is defending the vulnerable. What man has not been infuriated by injustice, exploitation, and oppression of the powerless and weak?

Randy did not understand the source of his anger and ended up turning that anger onto his own child. Once he was confronted with the truth, he was able to tame that anger, that energy, and use it to motivate positive changes in his parenting. Once he woke up in his father's shoes, he was able to gain a sense of understanding and experience a level of forgiveness. His anger turned from punishing his son to fueling a determination to protect his son from what he had suffered growing up.

Taking Charge

I'd like you to ask yourself some questions about your anger. There are no right or wrong answers here, so avoid trying to decide how you're "supposed to" respond. The only way this works is for you to be honest with yourself.

1. What did you learn about anger as a child?
2. How did you express anger as a child?
3. Describe your most recent "anger" experience.
4. Describe the angriest moment in your life.
5. List the variety of ways you deal with anger.
6. What pleasure do you get from anger?
7. Do you have positive ways you get rid of anger? How?
8. Have you ever used your anger as a weapon against others?
9. What is your definition of anger?
10. How do you know you're angry?

Next, I'd like you to do some fill in the blank statements that will help you discover the ways you use anger in your life.

Anger is _____

I get angry every time _____

I get angry whenever somebody _____

I get over anger quickly when _____

When I get angry, my face _____

Whenever I'm angry and I don't want anyone to know, I

_____

When I keep my anger inside, I _____

The best thing for me to do when I'm angry is to

_____

After I lose my temper, I _____

I feel my anger is _____

In this chapter, I mentioned a variety of ways that anger can manifest itself. I'm going to list several examples, and I'd like you to put a mark next to those that you recognize as ways you use to show your anger. I recognize this is a long list, but each man will use different methods as a way to release anger. It's important for you to know yourself.

- Volcanic and random verbal and/or physical outbursts
- A defensive posture and a tendency to "jump the gun" in defending yourself
- The need to be right in conversations and conflicts
- Attempting to control others by demands/commands
- Overusing sarcasm
- Using guilt to control the behavior of others
- Experiencing lack of joy in life and pleasure in daily activities
- Depending on sports as an "acceptable" way to show anger—either playing or watching
- Plotting and scheming against other people
- Speaking negatively about other people
- Being overly prideful and selfish
- Engaging in habitual sexual pursuit and conquest, including sexual jokes, innuendo, speech, and flirting behavior

- Procrastinating tasks you don't want to do
- Perpetual or habitual lateness
- Numbing out your feelings with alcohol or drugs
- Sarcasm, cynicism, or being overly critical
- Being overly polite, cheery on the outside but resentful on the inside
- Frequent sighing
- Withdrawing into your own "world" as a way to cope
- Overly controlled monotone voice
- Frequent disturbing or frightening dreams
- Spending money you don't have and buying things you don't need
- Difficulty getting to or staying asleep
- Being easily fatigued or apathetic
- Loss of enjoyment in everyday activities
- Getting irritable over small things
- Clenched jaws, fists, muscles
- Using threats of or actual physical violence against others
- Raising your voice incrementally
- Facial ticks, grinding teeth, spasmodic foot movements done unintentionally
- Stomach ulcers
- Using religious texts as a way to control, belittle, or shame others

In this chapter, I gave you three visuals for anger.

- The Slow Burn—anger always present but kept controlled
- The Flash Burn—anger that is quickly felt, of short duration, intensely experienced

- The Smoldering Coals—anger that catches you unawares in its presence and intensity

I'd like you to think about your own anger reactions in relation to these three. Which one best describes you? Are you a combination of one or more?

Each of these is an example of *unresolved* anger. These are examples of an anger that never really goes away. Unresolved anger becomes accumulated anger. The more anger you accumulate, the harder it is to control. Unresolved, accumulated anger has the multiplied power to overtake your best intentions and your efforts to change. Until that anger is confronted and worked through, it will continue to remain unresolved, growing greater in destructive strength. I've heard unresolved anger called the silent killer because of its damaging physical effects, and I believe repressed anger may be one of the reasons the life span of men in our culture is shorter than that of women. That stress, building and improperly vented, over years and years and years takes its toll on a man physically, emotionally, relationally, and spiritually.

Sometimes it's hard to know just how angry you are because you've been covering it over, denying it for years, calling anger something else, or blaming others. I'd like you to consider doing a little physical exercise to help. Go get a tennis ball or some small ball that isn't going to cause any real damage. What I'd like you to do is start out thinking about the things that irritate you; these could be getting cut off on the freeway or sales calls in the evening after dinner or that guy at work who keeps subtly putting you down. I'd like you to think about those things and throw the tennis ball up against a wall. It could be a wall at your house or apartment (hopefully one without a window unless you've got really good aim) or at a local park.

Start with the things that seem small or trivial and then allow your thoughts to flow to other things that have made you angry in the past and/or make you angry now. If it makes you angrier, throw the ball harder. As you throw the ball, connect to the anger, but don't just stop there. Now that the anger is out in the open, take a good look at it. Examine it from all sides—top, bottom, left, right. Where does it come from? Look at it and name it. By doing so, you will gain power over your anger. You'll recognize it better so the next time it flares up, you'll have a better shot at putting it into proper perspective.

Once you're done, I'd like you to consider something else. It's not enough to just throw a ball against a wall and get mad. To get a handle on your anger, you need to do more than just throw it around. Face it—just "throwing" your anger against other people is about as effective as throwing that ball against the wall. All it does is bounce right back at you. If that's what you've been doing for years, why not try a different strategy? Figure out your anger and turn it from something negative in your life to a way to motivate you toward something positive.

Anger is powerful, and negative anger is surely addictive. It's important for every man to understand how he relates to anger and be responsible for how he uses anger. If, after working through this Taking Charge section, you realize you have a problem with anger, I encourage you to seek out help and accountability. This could be as informal as talking about it with a good friend or as formal as getting professional counseling in anger management. If anger is negatively affecting your life, pretending it isn't an issue is not helpful for you or those you know and love. Keep the power but make it your own, for good, to shield not to wound, to protect not to punish, to make you a better man.

In this chapter, I gave you lots of examples of unhealthy anger. Before we go on to the next chapter, I'd like to leave you with just a few positive examples of what can happen when you're free from unhealthy anger in your life.

- *More peace.* Each day doesn't have to be a perpetual battle. Every man needs times of peace, times to strengthen, reflect, and grow. Battles in this life are inevitable, but the contests life throws at you are easier to win when you're not always fighting against yourself.

- *Emotional strength.* Don't buy into the lie that you're not an emotional being; you are. When you're free from the constant onslaught of anger, you're able to start noticing and experiencing the other emotions available to you as a man—joy, optimism, contentment, appreciation, gratitude, patience, and love.

- *Bonded relationships.* When your primary relationship in life is with anger, that doesn't leave much room for anything else. Remove all that rage, and your relationships will deepen and strengthen.

- *Better sleep.* Anger never leaves you alone; it never shuts up; it's always harping on you, needling you into action and reaction, even when you sleep. Deal with the anger, and you'll find your world is a lot quieter.

- *Greater impulse control.* Anger keeps you wound up tight, on edge and ready to snap. Freedom from unhealthy anger allows you to take a breath, think things through, respond instead of react.

- *Improved health.* When you're no longer being stalked by the silent killer, your body is going to be in better shape.

- *Less anxiety.* Being juiced up on anger leads to hypervigilance. When you're not so sure disaster is right around the corner, it won't be.

- *Less depression.* When you're no longer under siege by your rage, the world of your own thoughts and emotions becomes a safer place to venture into.
- *Substance free.* When you release anger, you remove a powerful motivator in the use of substances to "check out"—anything from alcohol and drugs to Twinkies and Ding Dongs.
- *Rediscovery of you.* You are more as a man than your pain and your anger. You have a vital, necessary role to play in the life of your family, friends, and co-workers. They need you to be more than just an angry man.

Reaching Higher

The Bible doesn't say anger is a sin. People get angry. God gets angry. But when people get angry for the wrong reasons, when they stay stuck in their anger, hurting themselves and others, that's the sin.

> Go ahead and be angry. You do well to be angry—but don't use your anger as fuel for revenge. And don't stay angry. Don't go to bed angry. Don't give the Devil that kind of foothold in your life.
>
> Ephesians 4:26–27 MSG

Anger is a natural reaction to pain, to injustice, to wrongness in the world. Our challenge as men is to keep control of our anger, to understand where it comes from and why it happens, and to be responsible for how we use it in our world.

4

Emotional Withdrawal

Don't get me wrong," David assured me. "I love my wife." The beautiful summer day had invited the two of us out for a walk instead of talking in my office. A slight breeze was blowing, and it felt good to be outside. As we headed away from the building, we touched base on some business news and how the local sports team was doing then moved on to harder topics. As David really started talking, he stopped focusing on the scenery. And the more animated he got, the quicker we walked. It was worth working up a sweat in the middle of the day to finally get him to open up. That was part of the issue in his marriage to Elaine—David's closed nature. Elaine was deeply hurt by what she termed his "lack of trust." She thought he was punishing her by refusing to share his thoughts, feelings, and emotions. The harder she pressed, the more withdrawn David became. She thought he was being obstinate. I wanted to hear what David had to say.

"Don't get me wrong. I love my wife, but sometimes she scares the crap out of me. She'll come at me, talking a mile a minute,

75

and I just feel like I'm drowning. She's so . . . intense, wanting to know why I did something or demanding I drop everything—right now—and listen to what she has to say. And then I'm supposed to respond immediately. If I don't, I'm the bad guy—all while I'm trying to figure out what I did wrong in the first place." He looked straight ahead. "It's like I'm being attacked."

David stopped talking but certainly didn't stop walking. He was clearly angry.

"What do you do when you're being attacked?" I asked, using his words.

"Sometimes I get so mad I want to yell at her to just stop talking," he said, exhaling loudly. "I did that a couple of times when we were first married, and it didn't go over very well."

"So what do you do now when you get mad?"

"Well, I can't yell . . . and throwing something across the room is out of the question." He smiled and looked over to see if I was going to respond to that last statement. When I just kept walking, he kept going. "My goal now is to get whatever it is over with as quickly as possible."

"How do you do that?"

"I just let her unload," he said matter-of-factly. "I don't try to defend myself anymore. She's much better at prosecuting than I am at defending. I mean, she brings in stuff I did or said three years ago—like I even remember—and uses that against me. I just shut up and try to figure out what the real problem is so I can fix it. That way, I won't get unloaded on again, at least not for the same thing."

We kept walking in silence for a bit, and then I asked, "Have you ever told Elaine she scares you when she gets this way?"

That stopped him in his tracks. "Are you kidding? Why would I want to do that?"

Under Siege

We live in a world inundated by visual and emotional stimuli. People, events, and technology all clamor for our attention. *Look over here! Look over there! Buy this! Buy that! Change this! Change that! Stop this! Start that!* We listen to talk all day long—from the people around us, from the media, from the voices inside our heads. Those voices constantly jab and poke at us, prodding us into action or reaction. We can feel deluged in all that chatter. We can feel goaded into responding before we're ready.

All of this activity produces stress. From getting out the door so you can get to work on time, to completing the project at work, to communicating with co-workers about that project, to keeping track of the myriad ways people have to demand your attention, you can feel very overwhelmed. Add to that the stress of realistic and unrealistic expectations about who you are and who you're supposed to be from yourself, your family, and others, and each day can be a sort of assault on a man's sense of competency and worth.

Don't get me wrong—for all of that, I'm generally up for the challenge. If it's me against the world, I say "Look out, world!" But I have to admit there are days when it seems like the world has the upper hand. On those days, I find myself needing to "get away from it all" in order to have some space to think and plan and recharge.

It was in John Gray's book *Men Are from Mars, Women Are from Venus* where I first heard the term "cave dwell." According-ing to Gray, men cave dwell; they withdraw in order to process actions and reactions, for emotional safety and protection. Men withdraw for a variety of reasons, and they also have a variety of ways to withdraw. I've known men who literally did cave dwell. They would come home and retreat into an office or den, some-place dark and quiet—their own little "cave." I've known men

77

who would use the garage as their cave, immersing themselves in a project as a way to tune out the rest of the world and its demands. Some men play sports, others play video games; some surf the internet, others watch television. You know a man is cave dwelling when he puts up that invisible but very evident sign that says "occupied."

Men can also cave dwell or withdraw when they feel threatened. David felt threatened by Elaine, so he chose the "flight" part of the fight-or-flight response to stress. Under siege, David decided to check out. The more Elaine demanded him to engage, the more determined he was to withdraw. The more he withdrew, the more Elaine began to look at him as someone foreign, someone she couldn't understand. Without knowing what David was feeling, she began to assign negative motivations to him. Elaine thought David didn't love her when he withdrew. But David was simply trying to protect his love for her, having experienced the downside of full-on "engagement" with her early in their marriage. This miscommunication was playing a significant role in their marital discord.

John Gray's book came as a revelation to Elaine. It never dawned on her that David's thoughts, reactions, and responses would be so different from her own. She didn't realize that David needed emotional space where he could reset, renew, and restore. She hadn't contemplated the metaphor that she and David were from different "planets" and needed to relearn how to communicate with each other. Elaine was able to start seeing David's reactions as part of his maleness and not take it personally. She also learned how and when to approach David when she needed to talk through something. Once the lightbulb clicked for Elaine, she attacked the situation with the same sort of tenacity and intensity David had talked about on our walk.

Courage and Exposure

Most men need their downtime, their cave dwelling, where they can get away and appear to be thinking about nothing at all as a way to process and place situations and feelings into perspective. It is like men have a very necessary Nothing Box in their brain, where they need to go and recharge. Women use talking as a filter for reflection, but most men require times without talking—times of doing—in order to reflect. It's as if by *not* concentrating on a difficult problem, they have a better chance of solving it. A little time away is, therefore, not a bad thing for men. The question becomes, of course, how much of a good thing turns it into a bad thing.

Men run the gamut between extreme revealers and extreme concealers. Extreme revealers make sure everyone knows what they're thinking at all times, whether that knowledge is requested or not. They live as an open book written in large, bold print. Extreme concealers are the opposite. Their intention is to make sure to keep what they think, and even their personality, hidden. This hiding in plain sight is used as an angry or fearful shield against a perceived hostile world. When this concealment becomes entwined around their personality, it can be difficult to unravel the reasons and to coax them back out into the light.

Some men withdraw from others as a continuation of a survival strategy from childhood. Perhaps they grew up in a household where one or more parent was highly verbal, intense, and opinionated, a household typified by this sign I once read: "Everyone is entitled to their own opinion, as long as it agrees with mine." Perhaps they realized no one really cared what they thought, what they wanted or needed, so they withdrew into themselves to meet their own needs. Perhaps the anger they felt at being marginalized or devalued or dismissed or simply ignored was so great that they chose to nourish that anger in secret.

It is my experience that extreme emotional withdrawal rarely comes without a component of anger and/or fear. After all, fight or flight happens when a person feels threatened. In response to a threat, the reactions of anger or fear or both are quite common.

When David said Elaine scared him, he wasn't being rhetorical—she did. Her emotionally intense verbal outbursts were highly reminiscent of his mother. David loved his mother, but he spent a good portion of his childhood terrified of her. He never knew what would set her off, though her anger always seemed to center on some fault of his. David's mother wasn't just angry with him, she was also disappointed in whatever way he was found to be lacking. She was much more tolerant of David's younger sister and seemed to unload her highest level of displeasure in his direction. David wanted very much to please her and was devastated that he so often fell short.

In response to her volatility, David withdrew into himself. He stayed in his room as much as he could. He learned to keep his head down, his eyes averted, and to speak in a carefully modulated voice so he couldn't be accused of "back talking." The older he got, the more enraged at his mother he became, but because he was so repulsed by the depth and intensity of her outbursts, he made a decision never to show how hurt or angry she made him in return. David became a stoic child and a sullen adolescent.

What started out as a strategy in childhood continued as a habit in adulthood. As Elaine began to moderate her interactions with David based on what she was learning, she expected that he would adjust also, but that didn't happen. David opened up a little but continued his pattern of avoidance and withdrawal. It was time to take another walk.

At the point when Elaine and David reached this impasse, fall had definitely settled into the air. Grabbing our coats, he and I headed out again, with me wishing I'd had the foresight to bring along a hat because of the chill wind blowing off the water just a few blocks away.

"Elaine's getting frustrated," I told David. "She's trying very hard to adjust her own behavior toward you and can't understand why you're not reciprocating." He didn't say anything and kept walking.

"What's the problem? Why are you holding back? She just wants to know what you're thinking."

There was still no response, which gave me some idea of what Elaine was going through.

"You say you love your wife, right?" I asked, to which David merely nodded his head. "Okay, you love her, but do you trust her?"

That caught his attention. "What do you mean, 'do you trust her'?" he shot back, agitated. "You think she's seeing someone else?"

"No, that's not what I'm talking about. Do you trust your wife enough to let her see who you really are?"

Again, silence. I knew that concept was going to take a block or two.

"So you think I'm afraid to show Elaine who I really am, and that's why I'm so closed all the time?" I couldn't tell if he was making a statement or asking a question.

I let what he said just sort of hang there in the wind before I asked, "Do you remember the last time we did this and you said you were scared of Elaine?"

"Yeah, but we worked through that. It was because of the way she came at me back then."

"True, and according to you and her, she's changed over the past couple of months, but you really haven't. I was just wondering why that could be."

"You think it has to do with trust?" I could tell he wasn't really buying my theory.

"I'm wondering if you're still scared, not of Elaine this time but of yourself."

"I'm not following you at all." His voice was flat and slightly confrontational.

"When was the last time you really opened up to somebody?"

"To you—over the summer." Even though he didn't say it, it was obvious he was thinking, *And look where it got me.*

"I'd like you to consider if you're still afraid when you talk to Elaine—afraid to show who you really are, what you really think and feel. Could it be that you think Elaine loves you *in spite of* who you are instead of *for* who you are?"

David stopped walking and closed his eyes before he said, "How can she really love me when she's always finding so many things about me that are wrong?" His voice sounded tired and dejected.

"Okay. You love her, but you don't trust her to love you back."

"Yeah, I guess that's right," he said, and he didn't look happy.

Men can find it difficult to open up to others because of an intense fear of rejection. They are afraid opening up will provide a chink in their armor, a narrow opening to a vulnerable area that could be used against them. They're afraid if they let others in, those people will uncover some hidden weakness or fault. Men project a sort of bravado to the world but can harbor deep-seated fears about their ability to measure up. Staying closed down, refusing to let anyone in, can become a way to protect against exposure.

Women tend to do the opposite; they talk about their fears and process them with others. Men, however, like to slay their own dragons. With men, the greater the potential for exposure, the greater the need to protect and to stay hidden. The very things Elaine wanted David to open up about—to demonstrate his love for her—were the very things David wanted to keep hidden, to protect her love for him.

Other people, especially women, do not want the men they love to stay hidden. A hidden man is an inaccessible man; a hidden man is a suspicious man. A woman's capacity for understanding, empathy, and forgiveness is often greater than her capacity for being "left in the dark." She'd rather know what you're thinking. I recognize that not every man reading this chapter will be married, but most will have a mother, a daughter, a sister, an aunt, and female co-workers and acquaintances. In order to maintain healthy relationships with the other half of the population, you need to get used to a little risk and exposure. Call it an Adventure in Honesty.

You don't have to spill your guts to total strangers, but consider how open and accessible you are to those around you, not only to the females in your life but also to the males. Developing a habit of emotional withdrawal leaves you incommunicado to both sexes. There may be brothers or sons or fathers or friends who would benefit from the gift of knowing you better.

Taking Charge

I'd like you to envision a wall made out of bricks. You can think of it in your mind or draw it on paper. If you're going to draw it, start with three bricks high and three bricks wide. Place yourself on one side of the wall and place "the world" on the other side of that wall. Now, I want you to label each brick with something you do—some activity you engage in, some behavior you exhibit—that constitutes part of that wall you use to keep others out. You might put not returning phone calls or reading the paper or working on your car. You could put keeping your shades drawn or using sarcasm or never volunteering for anything. How do you protect yourself from the demands of the world? What do you do when you feel under siege? It's vital you know your pattern.

When you're through with that exercise, I'd like you to think of the "caves" you've created—places where you can go and be alone. Perhaps it's your den or garage, like we talked about earlier. Maybe it's a hiking or running trail or a weight room. Maybe it's a certain television show, video game, or sports programming. Where are your caves?

Now that you've got those visuals, answer these questions:

- What's the first cave you can remember?
- What sent you there in the first place?
- How often do you find yourself withdrawing into your cave of choice?
- How long do you need to be "offline" before you're ready to get back in the game?
- What stresses today trigger you to head to the cave?
- Is there a particular time of day or day of the week when you're more tempted to check out?
- When you're in your cave, how do you react when asked to leave?
- What's the longest you've spent truly alone in your life?
- Of all the secrets you hold close, which is the one that frightens you the most?
- Of all the secrets you hold close, which one do you make sure you never reveal?
- When was the last time you were completely honest with someone? Who was it and why did you share what you did?
- Who are the people you hide from the most?

- Who are the people you love the most? Compare and contrast your answers above.
- In order to open up to another person, what do you need in place first?
- Are you someone who is able to hear the secrets of others?
- Are you someone who is trustworthy with the secrets of others?
- What is more important to you—to be respected or to be known for who you are?
- Do you think it's impossible for people to love you (or respect you, like you, trust you) if they know who you really are and what you really think? Complete the question using each of the words in parentheses.
- What is your definition of courage?
- Are you a strong enough person to let others see your faults?

There is no shame in admitting weakness when the admission is the truth. Admitting weakness allows you to accept its presence in your life, but acceptance doesn't need to be the end of the story. Many men are uncomfortable confronting their own weaknesses, so those weaknesses continue to cause problems. In order to flee from those overwhelming feelings, men isolate themselves. This isolation breeds an island mentality, a sense of loneliness. Lonely men often choose destructive companions like addictions. As addictions gain strength, so does despair. Despair leads to a sense of hopelessness and no exit. Be careful of caves, or you may find yourself in one with no clear or easy way out.

Weaknesses can grow in strength and impact. Before long, you've given that weakness the strength of a dragon. Instead of confronting it and bringing it out in the open, you keep it hidden and nurture it in secret. Maybe it's time to stop feeding the dragon and start slaying it. There are families to save and homes to protect and, in David's case, damsels to be won.

Getting in touch with how you're doing emotionally doesn't mean you need to turn into someone who tears up at chick flicks or who unloads every time someone asks how you're doing. What it does mean is being courageous enough to take stock of how you're doing inside, to face it and fix it when needed. As you become more comfortable with who you are, you'll likely find it easier to share that person with others.

Most people want to get to know you—not so they can attack you but because they're genuinely interested in who you are as a person. With other men, you can engage in a variety of activities that will demonstrate who you are, mostly through doing but sometimes through talking. It's probably going to be the other way around with the women in your life—some doing but mostly talking. Doing and talking, talking and doing are needed to engage in that complex engagement called relationship. You might be surprised by how many people are in your life right now who are waiting for you to come out and fully engage.

Reaching Higher

There is someone who already knows you better than you know yourself. That someone is the One who created you. You cannot run from him; he's everywhere, in every cave and hiding place you devise.

> God, investigate my life; get all the facts firsthand.
>> I'm an open book to you;
>>> even from a distance, you know what I'm thinking.
>> You know when I leave and when I get back;
>>> I'm never out of your sight.

You know everything I'm going to say
    before I start the first sentence.
I look behind me and you're there,
        then up ahead and you're there, too—
    your reassuring presence, coming and going.
This is too much, too wonderful—
    I can't take it all in!

Is there anyplace I can go to avoid your Spirit?
        to be out of your sight?
If I climb to the sky, you're there!
        If I go underground, you're there!
If I flew on morning's wings
    to the far western horizon,
You'd find me in a minute—
    you're already there waiting!
Then I said to myself, "Oh, he even sees me in the dark!
    At night I'm immersed in the light!"
It's a fact: darkness isn't dark to you;
    night and day, darkness and light, they're all the
        same to you.

Psalm 139:1–12 MSG

Did you notice the line that said "your reassuring presence"? For some men, God's presence is anything but reassuring. I hope that's not you, but it might be, because some men not only hide from others and themselves but also desperately try to hide from God. Well, you can't, nor should you. Not because it's a useless gesture in the first place because he's everywhere, though that's certainly true. You shouldn't hide from God because he loves you. When you hide from God, you hide from love.

God is not like an earthly father, whose ability to love is damaged by life and experiences and circumstances. God is your

heavenly Father, perfectly able to know everything about you—
more than you know about yourself—and still deeply, passion-
ately, with ultimate commitment, love you. If you're running
from him, it's time to stop. If you're hiding from him, it's time to
come out.

5

Work

This chapter is one of the hardest for me because I lived the life of 24/7 work for the first ten years of my practice. I was always at work. Work was where my life was most meaningful and energized. At that point, I had no children, and my wife, LaFon, worked right alongside me in the business. In a way, the business was like our child, and we put everything we had into watching it develop and grow. We started right out of graduate school, in a small storefront off the state highway. After a couple of years, we moved to a larger office, with more space and more people coming on board to help with our mission. We worked nights and weekends with the best of intentions. Work, though, was never done. It was just paused for things like eating and sleeping and church on Sundays. I didn't take vacations, and time off was measured in hours, not days or weeks. I felt guilty for taking time off and guilty for not *wanting* to take time off.

I had no time for anyone other than the people I was dealing with through my practice. The only way my friends could spend time with me was by booking an appointment. I literally worked them in between the depressed mother of four at one o'clock and the men's anger group at three. It was out of control; I was out of control. I spent all my time helping others find balance, perspective, and insight—and found myself totally missing the mark.

Those early years, though, were heady and exciting. They combined the secular bang of business success with the spiritual high of mission and ministry. Each day, each hour held the potential for another win, so I just kept going and going, day after day, week after week, year after year. Such a pace was impossible to maintain, of course. In my race to help others, I reached a point where I was exhausted, dispirited, and burned out. The people who before had given me such a jolt of energy I now saw as draining the very life out of me. I began to resent them and the work and the demands.

The business was doing great, but I was not. I needed to find my way back to the balance and peace I so desperately wanted to help others find. My journey from the abyss of burnout became the book *Becoming Strong Again: How to Regain Emotional Health*. That book, published in 1998, resonated so strongly that it came out with a new title and a new name, *How To De-Stress Your Life*, a decade later in 2008.

I say all this as a way to be honest about what I've gone through in my own life. I'm not proud of many of the choices I made back then. To this day, I regret the stress and pressure I put on myself, my friends, my family, and most especially my wife. What I do not regret, however, are the valuable lessons I learned when I came to my senses and began to look at myself and my life from a more balanced perspective. I consider every personal shortcoming, every painful life lesson of value. An understanding of my own nature and shortcomings increases my insight and compassion for other people. What I experienced gives me an ability to see down the road where others are going, to sound a warning and point out a different direction. Work can be a personal pinnacle, but you need to be careful of lofty heights. Pinnacles and towers can elevate, but they can also become prisons. When work becomes your life, work steals your life.

What You Do

In our culture, we use code words all the time. We meet an acquaintance or even someone new, shake hands, and say, "How are you?" That's code for "I'm just being polite." We don't really want a recitation of how that person's doing. In fact, it's fairly awkward if the person says something other than the standard code response of "good" or "fine." Unless the person is a close friend, hearing the words "lousy" or "not good at all" can derail a casual conversation pretty fast. As soon as you can, you're making excuses and saying things like, "Look at the time . . ." or "Well, I gotta go . . ."

Work has become a sort of code also. Think about what you say when you first meet another person, especially another man. How soon is it before you ask that man what he does? You want to know what sort of work he engages in. What he does helps you decode who he is. Who he is helps determine how you relate to him and how you think he might mesh with you.

Have you ever watched one of those nature programs where they show rams locking horns and pushing off against each other? I saw something similar the other day, only this was at a social gathering, during the cocktail hour before dinner. Many of the people in the room were new to each other, being brought together at this fundraiser for a local charity. The two men started out by shaking hands and establishing territory through the code phrase, "So, what do you do?" It always surprises me how everyone seems to understand what this question refers to. Occasionally someone will mention the word *work* or will expand the question to, "So, what do you do for a living?" but usually just the simple "What do you do?" is understood as an inquiry into what sort of work you do.

In our culture, you are defined by your work. It's not that way in other cultures. In other cultures, you are defined by your family and your place within that family. They don't ask "What do you do?" they ask "Who's your father?" or they want to know if you're the first or second born and about your mother's family. In a way, that makes a lot of sense if you live in a stable community without population shifts or huge influxes of new people. Our culture, however, is not stable; it's highly transitory. People move around a great deal and families can live long distances apart, so you exist as a separate individual, outside of a larger family context. In this type of environment, it's not surprising that family is no longer what determines the size of your horns. Still, horns are important, so we've merely switched how we measure them.

I listened to these two men size up the competition as they talked about their jobs, who they knew in the business community, the amount of success each was currently experiencing, and their future prospects. It was a cordial, though competitive, exchange, with each man emphasizing the positives and minimizing the negatives. As far as I could tell, it was successful because it ended with them trading business cards before their wives arrived to gather them up for dinner.

I'm often amused by the reactions I get when it comes to this code of work-for-worth. When I tell women I'm a therapist, they'll generally perk up and be very interested. Women represent the overwhelming percentage of people who utilize counselors (notice I said "utilize" not "need"). Women traditionally have assigned value to therapy. It hasn't been that way for men. In the past when I'd explain I'm a therapist to other men, the response has been either a glazed-over look of *Why would you want to do that?* or a sort of veiled antipathy of *Oh, you're one of those guys.* I've gotten to the point now where I start out by saying I'm a business owner, an author, and a speaker. I let that sink in a bit and then mention the nature of my practice because, when it comes to other men, that helps with the size of my horns.

Work as Worth

I learned something interesting about work back when I first started my business. I learned that work was different from the other major life endeavor I'd undertaken—academics. In school, there was always a time when classes were over, when tests were taken, diplomas awarded. Work, however, is never done. There is always one more email to write, phone call to answer, account to be balanced, procedure to be tweaked, and always one more person to be helped. The needs of a business are never satisfied and are as elusive as vapor.

For ten years, I chased after that vapor, trying to nail it down. I tried so hard to get to a point where the business was "enough," to wrestle it to the ground and hear it say "uncle," but I never could and it never did. In the end, it was me who was ready to throw in the towel. I had to find a way to detach my sense of self from both my accomplishments and my failures. I'll admit that part of my drive to succeed had to do with a desire for recognition. Another part had to do with the price of failure. I agonized over every person who left my office unchanged, every unresolved conflict, every miscommunication I should have avoided, every unconnected dot that resulted in someone's continued pain. At the end of a day of successes, I stayed awake over those failures.

I got out of school thinking I should know more than I did, be more effective than I was, bring about more real change than was possible, sooner than was reasonable. In short, I set myself up for failure. When I succeeded, I felt great about myself. When I failed, I felt terrible about myself. I fell into the work-as-worth trap, and it took me ten years to climb out. So I understand this pit. Now I'm able to help other men recognize the trap and figure out their own way to freedom.

Just because work-as-worth can be a trap, it does not mean work has no worth. It does. Your job and the effort you put into it are very worthwhile. Your role as provider through your work is extremely valuable. However, your job, while valuable, does not constitute your total value as a person. Your job, while worthwhile, is not worth everything you have. Your job is not worth your relationships; it is not worth your health; it is not worth your sense of self. Work itself is worthwhile, but men can sometimes translate that into thinking their job is everything they are and have.

That was the box Jerry put himself in. The owner of a successful construction company, he'd taken great pride in having his name on the front door. Before the housing market cratered, Jerry had taken a big risk and gobbled up several development sites. He'd taken risks like this before and had always come out ahead. In fact, that was one of the things he'd loved best about his business—turning other people's failures into personal successes. He had no context for his own failure when the bottom fell out of both the housing market and his bank account. He narrowly avoided bankruptcy but was left with a shuttered business and few remaining assets. He and his wife went back to living in the smaller house they'd bought decades earlier and had been renting out. All of that work, all of that time, all the things he'd sacrificed for were gone. And with the business gone, Jerry lost sight of himself. If you'd asked him what he did, he would have no answer.

Jerry had to move from the construction business to the re-construction business. Jerry is reconstructing his life, his value, his worth. He's rediscovering who he is when his name isn't on the door or printed in gold on business cards. He's rediscovering other roles in his life that got pushed aside in the pursuit of his work.

Instead of being devastated by the loss of the company, Jerry's wife is stronger than he would have believed. The bigger the company got, the more it became Jerry's and the less it became hers. She says having it gone makes their life more like it was when they first started, with the two of them as partners in life. Jerry thought she loved him for all the things he was able to provide for her. Now he knows she just loves him. That's helping Jerry put the pieces of how he sees himself back together.

What you do cannot be the measure of who you are. Accomplishments come in all areas of life, not just in the world of work. I know men whose businesses are thriving, but their families are not. Their health is not. Their sense of peace and contentment is not. As men, we are workers, yes, but we are also fathers and brothers and sons. We are community leaders and soccer coaches. We are church deacons and neighbors. Is your job important? Yes. But I contend that your work is more important for how you do it than for what it is. How you do your work defines your character as a man, and character should really be how horns are measured.

Rat Race

Not everyone gets to be the owner of a company. That job is for a relative few. Most men work for someone else. They go in and are expected to be on time, to work late, and to do what other people tell them to do. For some of these workers, their jobs are not a positive place for completing tasks and competing against their best and the best in others to raise their game. Instead of work giving them a positive identity, these men feel trapped, resentful of the necessity of work, angry over the job they have, and fearful of change. They work because they have to, not because they want to. Instead of gaining too great a sense of self through work, they gain too little.

I have no idea where the term rat race started, but if I had to guess, I would say that the term originated from someone watching a swarm of workers either entering or leaving high-rise office buildings at the beginning or end of the day. The term rat race seems fixed within an urban setting, with swarms of workers caught up in the corporate momentum, moving more as a crowd and less as a matter of personal decision. Rat race is a picture of nondescript cubicles, with interchangeable parts—desks, computers, chairs, and those who sit in the chairs.

For me, rat race conjures up two images, neither very complimentary. The first is of rats running against each other in a maze. The maze is an artificial competition whose course and complexity is determined by others. The rat has no choice but to complete the maze as best he can; he either gets punished if he doesn't or rewarded if he does. But those consequences, the good and the bad, are determined by someone else. The second image of rat race that comes to mind is the proverbial rat in a cage, running on one of those rodent wheels. The rat is running his little heart out, constantly in motion but going nowhere. He's running and running and running, but he's still trapped inside of a cage.

Some men feel like rats when it comes to their jobs. They feel like one of the vast colony, scurrying to and from work on someone else's schedule, propelled along by mindless momentum, fearful of what will happen if they stop. They feel as if they're being pitted against others in an artificial environment where someone else determines and dispenses the rewards and punishments. They feel as if they're exhausting themselves each day, trying harder and harder to achieve but still going nowhere. Then, work becomes a mindless activity, something to be tolerated instead of a challenge to be overcome.

Men who feel like nothing more than rats, in my experience, tend to move in and out of jobs. They keep looking for the one job that will finally give them everything they're looking for, whether it's money or recognition or acceptance. When things don't go well, they tend to blame the job—the work itself, their supervisor, their co-workers, the conditions at the workplace. For these men, work can become as all-consuming as it does for the most successful CEO.

All-consuming work—whether we are constantly striving for success or repeatedly running from failure—is not healthy. There needs to be a balance and an appropriate place for work within our understanding of ourselves as men. Work within healthy boundaries can be a place where we test ourselves, so we can find a way to learn, adapt, and grow stronger. Then, the lessons we learn at work can be applied to our lives. When we do that, work is integrated into our lives in a healthy, balanced way.

The work you do—whatever it is—needs to be done to the best of your ability within the confines of where it fits with the rest of your life's obligations and responsibilities. If you're a CEO of a Fortune 500 company, do your job well, be a good example to others, and keep your work obligations balanced with your other responsibilities. It's the same if you're a server in a restaurant, a dentist, a bus driver, an architect, or a landscaper. There will always be aspects of your work—whether you're the boss or the busboy—that are solidly out of your control, but you hold the keys to your own responses, actions, and behaviors.

Taking Charge

For better or worse, there will always be a part of us as men that views ourselves and each other through the lens of work. Our challenge is to learn to look at ourselves and others from multiple views instead of a single focus. In order to do that, I'd like you to consider the different "hats" you wear in your life.

Most men have a variety of baseball-type caps. I have a stack of them myself. Grab a bunch of these hats and a handful of spare coins for this exercise. Using your hats, designate one hat for each of your functions—"worker," "father," "son," "husband," "friend," or "coach."

You can complete this hat exercise two different ways:

1. Thinking about where you get your greatest to your least sense of self-worth, line up your hats to match, with the hat providing the greatest sense of self-worth being in the front and the hat providing the least being in the back.
2. Taking your coins, consider how much energy and time you give and the value you place on each of your hats. Be honest and go through your handful of change, tossing the highest-value coins in the highest-value hat. You can also use the coins to indicate the time you devote to each hat. When you've run out of coins, take a look and see how "valuable" each hat is.

If you're brave, do this exercise with members of your family or friends who know you well. You might be surprised how others view you, your hats, and what you value.

Evaluate where you're getting your greatest sense of value and worth. I would venture to guess that whichever "hat" is first in line or holds the most coins is the one you give priority to in the way of time, energy, and attention.

Ask yourself:

Do these reflect the priorities I really want to have?

Where does my work fit in? Do I give it too much value or too little?

How would the people I care about move around my hats? Where do they fit into my sense of value?

These are not easy questions to answer, and this exercise may be one that doesn't immediately provide an "aha" moment for you. You might have to wrestle with this one awhile, and that's okay. Keep your hats handy, because we'll use them a little later on.

Reaching Higher

Jesus, in Luke 12:16–21 (MSG), tells a story about a successful businessman:

> The farm of a rich man produced a terrific crop. He talked to himself: "What can I do? My barn isn't big enough for this harvest." Then he said, "Here's what I'll do: I'll tear down my barns and build bigger ones. Then I'll gather in all my grain and goods and I'll say to myself, Self, you've done well! You've got it made and can now retire. Take it easy and have the time of your life!"
>
> Just then God showed up and said, "Fool! Tonight you die. And your barnful of goods—who gets it?"

That's what happens when you fill your barn with Self and not with God.

In my life, I had to face the truth that a part of my motivation for working so hard, for exchanging so much of my life for my business, was because I was filling my barn with Self and not with God. God never asked me to go that hard or give up that much; it was my decision, and I suffered the consequences, along with my family. I spent so much time working for tomorrow, I neglected to really live for today.

Work is good and meaningful, but it is only a portion of what makes up this life God gives us, a life that can be gone tomorrow no matter how much or how little money we have.

King Solomon, in Ecclesiastes 5:13–20 (MSG) puts it this way:

> Here's a piece of bad luck I've seen happen:
> > A man hoards far more wealth than is good for him
> > And then loses it all in a bad business deal.
> > He fathered a child but hasn't a cent left to give him.
> > He arrived naked from the womb of his mother;
> > He'll leave in the same condition—with nothing.
> > This is bad luck, for sure—naked he came, naked he
> > > went.
> > So what was the point of working for a salary of
> > > smoke?
> > All for a miserable life spent in the dark?

After looking at the way things are on this earth, here's what I've decided is the best way to live: Take care of yourself, have a good time, and make the most of whatever job you have for as long as God gives you life. And that's about it. That's the human lot. Yes, we should make the most of what God gives, both the bounty and the capacity to enjoy it, accepting what's given and delighting in the work. It's God's gift! God deals out joy in the present, the now. It's useless to brood over how long we might live.

A balanced life neither despises nor enshrines work. A balanced life recognizes that value and worth, and rewards come from a variety of life's avenues, including but not exclusively work.

6

Escape

He's never home," Michelle told me plainly. "And when he is, he still isn't . . . really there. He's not really there for me or the kids." She said this with no emotion in her voice, as if she was stating a fact like the sky is blue or there are never enough shopping days between Thanksgiving and Christmas. To her, his behavior was an indisputable fact of life. To me, it was also a statement of abandonment.

I listened as she continued her dry recitation of Tuesday and Thursday softball practices in the spring and summer, with games either Saturday or Sunday. In the fall and winter, it was indoor soccer. When she complained about all the time involved, Jeff told her she was welcome to come to the games to spend time with him. I could tell by the look on her face that Michelle didn't consider this a viable option.

During the football season, Jeff had season tickets for home games and went to a bar down the street for away games with a group of his buddies. "I can go a full week without really *talking* to him, if you know what I mean," Michelle told me. I was reminded of the term "football widow," except the way she described it, her widowhood lasted longer than a single season.

After Jeff flatly refused to come into counseling with Michelle, I tried a different tack. I told him I completely understood and suggested we catch a ball game together instead. I presented it as a way for me to get to know him better. Clearly, this was not what Jeff expected from his wife's therapist. Intrigued, he agreed, as long as I paid. I have baseball season tickets myself, so I arranged to meet him for a night game the next time the team was in town.

Michelle signed a release to allow me to discuss what was going on in our counseling sessions, in case Jeff asked about it. "It's not like I haven't told him—multiple times—what I'm telling you," she said when I explained I would need the release to speak to him. Over the course of the game, however, we didn't spend much time talking about Michelle. Early on, I just acknowledged she was frustrated by aspects of their relationship and was trying to work through those frustrations. Mostly, we talked sports.

I didn't try to direct the conversation to any particular place but waited to see where Jeff would naturally go. All evening, he was cordial, but there was definitely a wall. It didn't come down until we were about to separate to our own cars after the game. It dropped just a little as he said he'd think about maybe coming in to see me—if it would help his wife. I just nodded, said okay, and left it at that.

I waited a couple of weeks before I asked again if Jeff would come in with Michelle for a session. This time, he said yes. At the end of that first joint session, he agreed to keep going; apparently it wasn't as terrible as he thought it would be. In order to avoid a conflict, Michelle agreed to switch to one of our female therapists for her own counseling so the two of them could continue with me as a couple.

That was some of the strangest couples' counseling I've ever done. Michelle, who had initiated all this in the first place, tended to quietly blend into the background during our sessions together, letting Jeff and his issues take the lead. She was quick to acknowledge her own faults and worked at not becoming hostile or defensive. It was as if, after being kept in the dark for so long as to who Jeff really was, she was content to sit on the sidelines and watch him open up. "I just want to be a safe place for you to be yourself," she told him.

Safe Places

This world can be an unsafe place for men. It is a world in which we are expected to assume the role of protector and provider. Yes, we have been taught to regard the women in our lives as equal partners, but there is also the innate understanding that, depending on circumstances, when push comes to shove, the buck should stop right here with us. Acceptance of this responsibility role requires maturity and no small measure of fortitude. It is a challenge most men meet head-on, willingly, for the good of those they love.

Assuming this role can also be a burden in the classic sense of that word—as something picked up and carried. Burdens require a willingness to pick them up and the strength to carry them. Some men aren't always so sure they're up to the task of either. When a man isn't sure about himself and his ability to carry that burden, the world becomes less safe. It can be terrifying to wake up every day feeling unsafe, unsure of yourself, fearful of what will happen next, what will be expected of you, and whether that expectation will end in success or failure.

There is a precipice that exists between adolescence and adulthood. In adolescence, you believe you can do anything; in adulthood, you realize that "anything" can include catastrophic failure. Once you cross over into adulthood, you become responsible for your own successes and your own defeats. Some men have great difficulty crossing over that precipice because of a deep-seated fear of inadequacy. After all, when you are responsible for your own choices, there's no one else to blame if the decisions you make turn out poorly.

Getting to call your own shots is a perk of adulthood; dealing with the outcome of those shots is a responsibility of adulthood. Some men want the perks but not the responsibility. This is tragically seen, for example, in the number of men who father children and then fail to provide for them.

This desire to remain at the cusp of adulthood has been called the Peter Pan syndrome after a book by the same name, *The Peter Pan Syndrome: Men Who Have Never Grown Up*, by Dr. Dan Kiley. It refers to men who choose to reject adult roles and responsibilities in order to remain grown-up adolescents. I'm a Disney kid, so the Disney version is the Peter Pan I remember, but before Peter Pan was a Disney movie, it was a 1904 play (and then 1911 novel) by J. M. Barrie entitled *Peter Pan; or, the Boy Who Wouldn't Grow Up*. Peter Pan lived in a world of perpetual play, with make-believe battles and adventures with pirates and mermaids, fairies and villains, called Neverland.

Today, Neverland could be called by the name of a sport or hobby, or whatever place of escape and play men run to when the real world, with its duties, responsibilities, and burdens, gets to be too much.

Please don't misunderstand and think I fail to recognize the age-old adage "All work and no play makes Jack a dull boy." I've seen *The Shining*; I understand where "no play" ends. I also understand there is a flip side to that adage: "All play and no work keeps Jack a boy, period."

That was sort of what Jeff was experiencing in his life. As the main breadwinner of the family throughout their marriage, Michelle felt Jeff's primary job should be as a support to her, in the ways she determined. Jeff felt emasculated by Michelle's business success and, by contrast, his failure to earn as much money as she did. A world in which everyone knew Michelle's horns were bigger than his was an unsafe world for Jeff. He retreated instead into a world of escape and play, primarily through sports.

After the kids arrived, Jeff felt he was being pressured into a Mr. Mom role he didn't want. The more pressure Michelle exerted, the more he withdrew into his sports and hobbies. The strained status quo would probably have continued longer if Jeff's parents hadn't decided to move several hours to the north. Jeff's mom, who had been watching the children, was no longer available for babysitting. The real world came rushing in, and Michelle decided the shift represented the perfect time for Jeff to "grow up" and stop the "playtime." Michelle expected Jeff to give up some of his after-hours activities so he could help deal with the kids. Jeff was terrified he'd lose the only identity where he felt strong and free and in control.

Michelle had to own up to her part in Jeff's perpetual decisions to escape. A pragmatic woman, she was able to grasp the consequences of her actions and attitudes that elevated herself and belittled Jeff. She wasn't happy with where they'd ended up as a couple but understood how many of her decisions over the years had gotten them there. To her credit, Michelle didn't try to force Jeff back into adulthood. This time, she didn't belittle him or bribe him or threaten him, as she admitted she had in the past. Staying quiet and listening to Jeff open up about his own fears and inadequacies helped her to see the part she'd played in creating an unsafe world for Jeff in their marriage. Being such a take-no-prisoners type of person herself, she failed to recognize that Jeff's reticence to join what she called "the adult world" wasn't entirely selfish but was often fear-based. Because Michelle loved him, she determined to find a way, as she said, to become his "safe place." Instead of always expecting Jeff to support her, Michelle was willing to find a way to support him to assume a greater responsibility role in their lives and marriage.

Come Out, Come Out, Wherever You Are

In the pleasures of our culture today, there are so many places for a man to hide. In the pressures of our culture today, there are so many reasons for a man to stay hidden. These pressures produce a tremendous amount of stress in men. Stress produces anxiety. In an attempt to reduce this anxiety, some men push back against the cultural expectation of assuming a responsibility role in life. Instead of embracing the challenge of caring for others, some men determine only to care for themselves or to allow others to care for them. This keeps a man escaping into adolescent behavior—a man with the aging body of an adult but the stagnant motivations and rationales of a teenager.

Mature men understand that this isn't a fair or safe world all the time. They expect the danger and prepare themselves, as much as possible, to meet it. By spending so much time in Neverland as an adult, Jeff risked losing out on the adventure of family. Determined to remain stuck in adolescence, he risked losing out on the childhoods of his own daughter and son.

Escape, however you do it, whether through adult sports leagues or fantasy football or internet video games, has a place in life. It is a place where men can set down the burden of responsibility for a while and just enjoy being a guy. It is a place to challenge yourself, to meet friends, to get away from your normal environment and get out in nature, to breathe deeply and enjoy being a man. Game-playing is a special place to go, but you can't live there. You have to leave that place and reenter the world of hats and duties and responsibilities. There is a time when adult responsibilities cry out "Come out, come out, wherever you are!" and, as a man, you need to respond.

A couple of chapters ago, we talked about men and cave dwelling. Cave dwelling occurs when a man needs to retreat from the pressures and responsibilities of life, as a way to recharge, revitalize, and renew. The goal of cave dwelling is to emerge refreshed and refocused, ready to take on life's challenges. What do you do, though, when you find yourself hesitant or unwilling to leave the cave? What do you do when the majority of your time is spent inside the cave rather than outside?

Jeff needed to come out of the caves in his life. He needed to squint in the bright light of truth and adjust his eyes to the reality of his world. Michelle made more money than he did, but that didn't mean she was more valuable or important. Hiding out and playing games with other men did not make him more of a man in her eyes; it made him less. Their children needed a father, someone who accepted the responsibility role of protector and provider, in all the unique and special ways Jeff had to offer his children as a man.

After working together for months, Jeff decided to hold on to his football season tickets in the fall and one adult softball league in the summer. Michelle decided to reconfigure her work responsibilities to be able to spend more time with the family. Together, they negotiated a way to divide up the child-care duties that made sense for them both. They've committed to planning a date night at least twice a month, one outing that Michelle chooses and one outing that's Jeff's call. Michelle is even learning how to play a video game, one of the car races that doesn't involve general mayhem and blowing things up. She's not very good, and she's learning to be okay with that.

Taking Charge

I've noticed an interesting difference between men and women when they get nostalgic. Women tend to wistfully remember that time when they lived at home as a child, when they were cared for and loved by their parents. It was a younger time of cuddles and hugs, of warmth and security. Men, on the other hand, tend to place the "golden years" of wistful remembrance closer to adolescence, with the power and strength of teenage masculinity. This was a time full of that heady feeling of autonomy but still a time when someone else was paying the freight.

What do you think of as the "golden years" for yourself? When you get nostalgic for the way things were? Describe it or draw it. How old were you? Why was it so special? What benefits do you ascribe to that time? Who provided those benefits?

I'd like you to go back to chapter 4 and look over again the caves you listed. After reading this chapter, can you think of some escapes you didn't list in chapter 4? If so, what are they?

I'd like you to take a piece of paper and draw a square in the middle, leaving room on the sides. This square represents your caves and escapes. Inside the square, list them all. Now, on the outside of the square, I want you to list all of the things you are trying to escape from when you spend too much time game-playing or cave dwelling.

Next, I'd like you to date each object on your paper. For the caves or escapes, indicate how long you've been using them or what age you started. I just want you to get a sense of time and how long these have been present in your life.

Once you've gotten this exercise done, I'd like you to repeat it, but this time I'd like you to think back to when you were a teenager. Draw the box and put in the caves and escapes you used back then. On the outside of that square, think back to all of the things you were trying to avoid back then.

Compare and contrast the two pages. What is the same and what is different? Can you see any patterns in behavior from then to now? Are there things outside your adult box that are really just substitutes of things that surround your teen box?

For another activity, I'd like you to get out a sheet of paper and fold it into thirds lengthwise. Take all the items inside your box and write them down as a list on the left side of the paper. They don't have to be in any particular order at this point. In the middle section, using just one or a couple of words, indicate what benefit that activity has for you. On the right-hand side of the paper, indicate how that activity makes you feel when you're doing it. For example, maybe one of your caves is working on your car in the garage. In the middle benefits column, you might say working on your own car saves money on repairs. That's certainly a valid benefit, especially seeing some of the invoices I've gotten over the years from mechanics. For the right-hand column, you might say that you feel competent and useful when you're able to do a job yourself and save money. Fair enough. However, I'd like you to go further. Working on your car allows you to feel competent and useful. What other responsibilities are you avoiding by working on your car so much of the time? Could those other responsibilities include those where you feel less competent and less useful? Working with cars, for example, is much easier sometimes than working with people. People are notoriously more difficult to "fix" than cars. It is important to know why you engage in Activity A, but you shouldn't overlook why you might be avoiding Activity B by spending so much time with Activity A.

Now that you've done that exercise with the games and hobbies you engage in, I'd like you to do it with the other "hats" you wear. If you can't remember what they are, go back and get out the caps you used in the previous chapter. You can use the back of the trifolded paper or do a new one, but on the left-hand side, list all your responsibility hats. In the middle section, indicate the benefits you derive from wearing those hats. On the right-hand side, indicate how you feel about yourself and the identity you give yourself when you wear each hat. Go ahead and physically put on each hat as you do this exercise.

For example, maybe one of the hats you wear is coach. In the middle, you put as benefits to being a coach that you get to spend more time with your child who is on the team and you're providing a service to the community by volunteering. Those are both great benefits but, again, don't stop there. On the right-hand side, really think about all the reasons you enjoy wearing that hat. You might also feel good about being a coach because you're the one in charge. Maybe calling the shots is difficult with some of the other hats you wear. For every good thing you're doing that goes out of balance, there is a reason. Use the right-hand column to help you identify the reason if one of your hats is on crooked.

As you look over both lists, ask yourself if there are other avenues in your life that do or could provide you with similar benefits outside of games or hobbies. I don't think you need to give up connecting to those benefits and those feelings about yourself that you tap into through your hobbies, activities, and games; I do think you should consider how to transfer some of those benefits and positive feelings about yourself over into the responsibility "hat" category.

If you've never watched the movie *Hook* with Robin Williams, I encourage you to do so. The film was released in 1991, so you may have seen it back then but vaguely remember it now. Either way, I urge you to go and watch it again. Granted, it's based on a children's story, but it's got some fairly good actors in it besides Robin Williams as Peter Pan—Dustin Hoffman as Hook, Maggie Smith as Wendy, Bob Hoskins as Smee, and Julia Roberts as Tinker Bell. Watch it with your kids if you need some cover, but when you do watch it, I'd like you to do so as both the adult you are and the child you were. Allow yourself to, for a moment, get lost in the film and its message that real-life, ultimately, is the greatest adventure.

Life, when you are fully engaged, *is* an adventure. Unlike the controlled, stop-and-reset world of some games, life continues on whether you're winning or losing. Games were created to mimic life, to test you in an artificial environment so you can prepare to face the real world and its ever-present challenges. When you refuse to come out of that artificial world and deal with life, you shortchange your growth as a person and maturity as a man. And you fail to provide for and protect those who need you—those who need you now and those you haven't yet met.

Reaching Higher

Life can be downright terrifying. Running away and escaping can sometimes seem like a reasonable course of action. In chapter 6 of 2 Kings, we read about a situation in which running away seemed reasonable. The king of the Arameans had mounted an ambush aimed at the king of Israel. The Israelite king, however, was able to avoid the ambush because he was warned away by God's prophet, Elisha. This ticked off the king of the Arameans, who sent a large battle contingent to find and capture Elisha. When Elisha's servant woke up in the morning and went outside, he saw a hostile army encircling the city. Aghast, the servant ran to Elisha and cried, "What should we do?" I imagine running away and hiding seemed a good option to the servant.

Elisha had no such plans and told his servant, "Don't be afraid. Those who are with us are more than are with them." I can imagine the servant looking around at himself and Elisha and saying, "That's two," and then looking up at the surrounding army and saying, "That's more than two." The problem was Elisha's servant didn't factor in every part of the equation. There was a vital component missing. Elisha then prayed to God and asked God to open up the eyes of his servant. When the servant's eyes were opened, "he looked and saw the hills full of horses and chariots of fire all around Elisha" (2 Kings 6:17). When we're missing out on the heavenly army arrayed on our behalf, we're missing a vital component.

Life is overwhelming when we fail to see the spiritual forces deployed on our behalf by our loving Commander-in-Chief. If Elisha's servant had ducked out, had run away and hidden, he probably would have survived, but he would have missed witnessing and participating in an astounding miracle and spiritual show of force. If you spend a good deal of your life hiding, you're obviously surviving, but what miracles are you missing out on? Maybe it's time to ask God to open up your eyes.

7

Deception

Tell me about your dad," I asked. It was probably our third time together, and I could tell by the "This Business Is Closed" sign on Scott's face that he was already tired of coming in once a week and talking for forty-five minutes. Since he looked less than forthcoming, I decided to direct the conversation, so I followed up with, "Is he still alive?"

"Oh yeah, he's alive," Scott replied readily enough. "He lives about fifteen minutes away from me."

"Do you see him much?"

He shrugged his shoulders and said, "I guess. It's mostly about the kids, you know. Mom babysits a lot . . . and we do the typical holiday and birthday thing."

Scott looked like that was enough, but I wasn't finished. "Do just . . . you and your dad get together?"

The look in his eyes indicated he was on to me, but he exhaled and said, "No, not really," as if that was the end of it. It wasn't.

I asked the obvious question: "Why not?"

Scott had a decision to make. He could continue to pretend this wasn't a substantive subject, or he could put aside his resistance to talking about his dad. Men, especially men who have a wounded father-son relationship, can attempt to paper over the deep hurt, frustration, and anger they experience when thinking about or talking about their fathers. The father-son relationship can be a definite sore spot. When it is, men will either attempt not to talk about it at all or try to give the appearance it's no big deal. They'll try to convey the impression that this wounded relationship doesn't really make that much difference in their lives now, that they're over it. Except, of course, they aren't.

One of the most fundamental relationships a man has is with his father, living or dead, available or unapproachable. This relationship gives structure and flesh to what it means to be a man through the modeling of father to son. However, none of us is a perfect model, and our children, especially our sons, bear the consequences of those imperfections. As a boy you likely yearned to idolize your dad as a superhero. You wanted to be like him and tried your hardest to do so. At some point, however, you figured out that your dad didn't always act like a superhero. You figured out your dad wasn't always right; you figured out sometimes he was wrong. He wasn't able to leap certain buildings or stop every speeding train. Your superhero of a dad started shrinking down to normal size. His superhero cape became tarnished, its luster stained by human weakness. You wanted to forgive him, but part of you was angry you could no longer look up to him as larger than life. The smaller your dad shrank in your eyes, the harder it was to forgive him. Over time, resentment and anger toward your dad for not living up to that larger-than-life expectation can grow until it creates a barrier in your relationship. You want him to admit he's just human and ask for forgiveness for the times he messed up as you were growing up. You want him to admit it, but you're afraid to talk about it. Since you can't seem to talk about the one thing with your dad that continues to bother you, you find yourself less willing to talk about much else. You find excuses not to be together, and the relationship drifts. Your dad is unwilling to budge and so are you. An impasse develops. You can't seem to do anything about it because you've decided the only way to make your relationship right is for your dad to make the first move, which he doesn't.

Because Scott didn't really want to talk about his dad, he responded to my question as to why they didn't spend time together with, "I don't know," spoken with a no-big-deal attitude.

"Do you like your dad?" I asked back, adopting his nonchalant tone.

Scott's reaction was immediate and tinged with anger. "Of course I love my dad. What kind of question is that?" I could tell Scott wanted to either get up and move around at best or get up and leave at worst.

"Scott, I didn't ask if you loved your dad; I asked if you liked him." At this point, he did get up, move to the window, and look out. I waited.

When he turned back around to face me, his expression was open and sad; he'd made his decision. "No," he admitted, "I haven't liked my dad for years."

Truth, Justice, and the American Way

Scott's problem with his dad had to do with the first tenet of being a superhero—at least according to Superman—truth. Scott's dad didn't tell the truth—he lied; he fudged; he spun; he excused; he rationalized; he blamed. Growing up, Scott wanted nothing more than to believe his dad. When he was little, he did. When his dad told him all the wonderful things they were going to do together, he believed. When those things didn't happen and Scott's dad explained it was because of other people and things and circumstances, he believed. When his father switched from job to job, often moving the family to different cities and different schools, always with a promise that the next move was going to be the best and last, Scott believed.

As Scott grew up, though, he began to see the tarnished cape. Scott's dad rarely followed through on any of his promises, to anyone. The excitement Scott felt as a child when his dad said "yes" faded into a suspicious "wait and see" caution. He did a lot of waiting and very little seeing. Scott began to suspect his dad said "yes" as a way of saying "not now," and "not now" as a way of saying "no."

When he was younger, Scott internalized this rejection as an indictment of himself as a son. If only he were good enough or smart enough or better at sports or whatever, then his dad would do what he promised and take the trips and play the games and spend the time. As he got older, Scott recognized his dad basically said whatever he could to get himself off the hook, whether it was true or not. At that point, his dad became undependable. Scott began to look elsewhere for stability and assurance in his life, but he never got over the sense of betrayal.

Scott carried around a deep well of anger and resentment toward his dad, even though he loved him and wanted to forgive him. When I asked him why it was so hard now, as an adult man, to forgive his father, Scott said it was because his father had never taken responsibility for the way he'd acted.

"He's never once owned up to any of that stuff. He's never once been straight about all of the lies. I was just a kid, and I grew up thinking there was something wrong with me, when it was he who had the problem. Who does that to his kid?" He was in full-fledged anger mode now, frustrated and hurt by his relationship with his dad and perplexed that it was still something he desperately wanted.

"Are you sure he never followed through with anything?" I asked.

"I don't know," he said, shaking his head. "Maybe he did on some little stuff. But if it was anything that took planning or effort or caused him inconvenience, there was always a reason why it couldn't or didn't happen. He never apologized or owned up to it. It would have been easier if he'd just said no and been done with it. He just kept stringing me along, like some stupid ass with a carrot on a stick."

"So, little stuff, yes, but big stuff, no."

"The only time he ever came through with something big was in high school, and it really didn't even count."

"What do you mean?"

"I wanted to get a car my senior year. The deal was I could get one if I got a job to pay for gas, insurance—the usual stuff. We were supposed to be out looking for one. Of course, by that time, I knew 'we' really meant 'me.' Carl, my buddy, knew I was looking, and he and his dad found an old Impala as part of an estate sale. We ended up buying it, and I drove that car all through college before it finally died on the side of the freeway."

"So, you did get your car."

"Yeah, but to this day, Dad tells the story as if he was the one who went looking and he's the one who found it. He still talks about how much he loved that car, but he didn't do anything. He takes credit for something he had nothing to do with! He does that all the time. He never owns up to the things he does and tries to take credit for the things he doesn't. It drives me nuts."

"And that's why you can't be around him, right?"

"Yep, that's pretty much it."

Spit Promises and Pinky Swears

Do you remember all the things you did as a kid to ensure truth and honesty? I remember spit shakes (where you both spit into your palm and then shake hands while reciting the promise). This was a serious ritual. As children, we knew the importance of telling and keeping the truth.

Truth was a little easier, in some ways, to get a handle on when you were a kid. Either Billy stole your pencil or he didn't. Either Sally spilled the milk or she didn't. Truth was a black-and-white proposition.

It didn't take long, however, for truth to go from black and white to shades of gray. Yes, Billy did steal your pencil, but it really was Billy's pencil that you took yesterday without anyone seeing. Yes, Sally did spill the milk, but only after you pushed her because you both wanted the same cookie. You learned that truth isn't always obvious the first time you yelled, "Mom! Johnnie hit me!" and Johnnie got punished, even though you pushed him first. Inside, even as a child, you knew what full truth was and that you could choose not to share it in its entirety; you realized you had the ability to gray-out truth to your advantage. You figured out you had that ability, and you figured out that others did also.

I believe that once you realize that the truth can be a fluid thing, you learn to value it even more, hence the spit promises and pinky swears. Even as a kid, you know truth is fragile and can be manipulated, so you come up with ways to try to nail down truth and make it stick. It's irritating when other kids don't tell the truth, but it can be downright frightening when adults don't. Kids intuitively know it's important for the adult people who have charge of them to tell the truth. Kids want this and want it badly, even when the truth is difficult.

When truth is withheld from children, they will go to great lengths to fill in that void, using childish reasons, motivations, and rationales, often ill-suited for adult complexities. Scott, once he caught on that what his father said was rarely true, began by blaming himself for the failure. As he got older, he blamed his dad. As he got even older, he began to blame himself again.

"You know the worst thing?" he asked me, several sessions later.

I could have come up with several options based on our discussions but decided not to. I shook my head.

"The worst thing is when I find myself doing the same thing with my own kids. That's not the kind of man I want to be."

Fighting Windmills

It seems an old-fashioned notion, but there was a time when people operated under the principle of "A man's word is as good as his bond." It was a time when handshakes and not twenty-page legal contracts sealed the deal. When I was growing up, that concept was part of the male lexicon of virtues along with integrity, honesty, and trustworthiness—all those attributes we learned as part of the Boy Scout Law. The actual quote—"An honest man's word is as good as his bond"—was penned by Miguel de Cervantes, the author of the quintessential book on fighting against windmills and other lost causes, *Don Quixote*. Sometimes, living a life of truth—the whole truth and nothing but the truth—can seem like a lost cause.

When you do tell the truth in this grayed-out culture, people can look at you like you're as crazy as Don Quixote. There just seems to be less and less incentive to be straightforward, to tell the truth and bear the consequences. The cleverer you become as an adult, the easier it is to manufacture a version of the truth that avoids casting yourself in an unflattering light. When surface becomes more important than substance, people hesitate to drop their masks. The challenge in such a culture is not to reveal the most truth but to create the largest mask. Masks are huge for men in business and social circles. Why? Because, for men, fake masks come with fake horns.

Deception is a dangerous compulsion for many men. Truth is often handled like a competition. If you can deceive me, then it's really my fault for not being able to figure out the truth. This is a case of the classic "Fool me once, shame on you; fool me twice, shame on me." If I "lose" the truth competition and fail to recognize the truth a second time, I'm to blame and you're off the hook. In this truth competition, the dishonest person is not inherently the loser.

That bothers me because, as a therapist, I'm kind of in the truth business. Believe me, I've played this truth-game frequently with men. Hostile to the whole process of counseling, they will do their best to keep the truth hidden. It becomes my job to ferret out the truth. If I do, I "win." If I win, they win too, because truth shouldn't be a game. We have heard and many times believed the line "truth hurts." The dirty little secret, though, is that dishonesty hurts worse.

Tangled Web

"Oh, what a tangled web we weave when first we practice to deceive!" So said the eighteenth-century Scottish novelist Walter Scott. The visual here is of a sticky, tangled mess of a spider's web that eventually entraps the very one who creates it through deception in the first place. Once you start down a path of deception, of graying out, of—let's just go ahead and say it—lying, it's difficult to get off that path.

Lying is extremely habit forming. Once a lie is told, it must be maintained, often with more lies. Each new lie necessitates additional lies to maintain it, and each subsequent lie requires even more lies. At some point, the weight of the lies, multiplying exponentially, collapses and allows the truth, albeit damaged, to emerge. Perhaps that is why the Shakespearean phrase "truth will out" continues to find expression.

Lying, unless it is pathological in nature, is a learned behavior. Scott had to admit he learned it from his dad. As much as he didn't want to pick up that habit, he had—not to the extent of his father's lies but enough to cause anger and frustration. As men, we have gone from passing along "your word as bond" messages to our sons to "get away with whatever you can." I'm reminded of the recent political and corporate scandals that have rocked this country and our economy and the tangled web of lies undergirding them all.

Honesty should not be taken lightly or seen as something only the weak or the foolish do. Becoming men of our word is a way to bring a little luster back to that superhero cape.

Taking Charge

The Josephson Institute Center for Youth Ethics (www.character counts.org) does a survey every two years, measuring the ethical character of teens. To say that teen ethics have deteriorated over the past twenty years would be putting it mildly. In their latest report, the Josephson Center found that one-third of high school students admitted to stealing from a store, half admitted cheating on a test, and over 40 percent admitted they lied to save money. As men, we may lie to ourselves and use phrases like "little white lies," but the truth of our behavior is seen in its effect on our children. We are passing on a skewed value system that is a far cry from the first tenet of the Boy Scout Law we learned as kids[4]:

A Scout is Trustworthy. A Scout tells the truth. He is honest, and he keeps his promises. People can depend on him.

As adults, we can try to dress up the truth to make it look like something else. We do this because the term *lie* is so black and white. We prefer the grayed-out tones of other terms. So I've gathered up some of those other terms, and I'd like you to consider how you incorporate any of these into your day-to-day life.

Dismiss	Falsify	Shift
Minimize	Hedge	Magnify
Distort	Invent	Marginalize
Evade	Misrepresent	
Fabricate	Misspeak	

Feel free to add any of your own that come to mind. Look at each word and come up with an example in your own life. This could be a single incident or a pattern of behavior. If you are brave, ask a loved one to do this with you in mind. Caution: chose a straight shooter or just do it yourself.

Consider your HQ—Honesty Quotient—for the following situations, with 5 being consistently honest and 1 being consistently dishonest:

Paying your taxes	HQ=____
Reporting your hours at work	HQ=____
Being truthful to other people in casual conversation	HQ=____
Recounting events/accomplishments from your past	HQ=____
Embellishing career or work details	HQ=____
Talking about events in your future	HQ=____
Reporting physical features like height and weight	HQ=____

Talking about your academic record   HQ=____
Recalling romantic relationships   HQ=____
Recounting your ability to hold your liquor   HQ=____
Being truthful about personal habits   HQ=____

As adults, we can shake our heads at the deteriorating ethics of teenagers, but are we really that much different? After all, these kids are learning this behavior somewhere. Look over the following scenarios that track along with the Josephson study, and ask yourself, *What would I do?*

Scenario #1: Stealing from a store

You've just gone into the hardware store to pick up a variety of items for a Saturday fix-it project. In truth, this is your third trip. You've been at it since 8:15 a.m., and it's now 2:30 p.m. You thought you'd be done hours ago but aren't because half the parts you bought this morning don't actually fit in the afternoon. Finally, you've gotten your third part for the same job and are walking toward your car at the far back edge of the parking lot. (Question: who goes to the hardware store on a Saturday afternoon? Answer: everybody.) Looking over your receipt and counting out your change, you realize that in all the swapping and exchanging with the cashier, you've ended up with an extra $20. What do you do?

Scenario #2: Cheating on a test

You're at work and are going for a promotion, but first you have to successfully complete a computerized exam to demonstrate your knowledge of the new position. You've studied—kind of—and figure you'll just wing it and see what happens. You get to the room with the testing station and sit down. As you're messing with the mouse and the desk pad, you realize there's a piece of paper underneath. Pulling it out, you see it's the notes from the person who apparently took the test before you. What do you do?

Scenario #3: Lying to save money

It's the end of March and you've put off Turbo Tax as long as you can. You already know you're not going to get any money back and are nervous that you might actually have to pay something. As you're calculating your car allowance, you inadvertently double the amount of write-off for car expenses. You don't realize the error until you've already efiled your tax return and are going over the results with your spouse. What do you do?

I recognize that some of you may be saying, "Wait a minute! This isn't just about lying, it's about stealing and cheating." That's true, but stealing and cheating—and then justifying either—is also lying. Self-deception can be used to justify all sorts of lousy behavior. It is only when you muster up the courage to face the truth, wherever it leads you and whatever it says about you, that you exhibit the fearless tenacity and bravery of a true Superman.

Reaching Higher

We live in a world of "maybe," of "I'll get back to you," of "probably," of "that should work." These phrases act as our escape routes when we really don't want our "yes" to be "yes." And we've gotten so used to people not telling the truth, it hardly fazes us anymore. It's why we demand legal contracts and start parsing words and determining a legal definition of the word *is*. It's hard to find someone who will simply tell the truth.

This penchant for hedging our bets is ancient and part of human nature. It's as old as the Garden of Eden, when God asked Adam if he'd eaten of the forbidden tree. Instead of just saying yes, Adam tried to spread the blame around by insisting "the woman you gave me made me do it." Lying, hedging, fudging the truth, these are all time-tested strategies, but there is a simpler, better way to live.

Jesus, in Matthew 5:37, said, "All you need to say is simply 'Yes' or 'No'; anything beyond this comes from the evil one." Another way to put this is "mean what you say and say what you mean." This kind of honesty is the way adult men should conduct themselves in the world.

8

Competition

I saw a bizarre story the other day from my own state of Washington. A thirty-eight-year-old man was arrested after forcing his sixteen-year-old daughter to compete in a duel, complete with armor, helmet, and wooden sword. He was angry she had gone to what he considered a crack house the night before, and apparently thought dueling would teach her a lesson. According to the story, however, he first sat on her while he beat her with willow branches (he's reportedly three hundred pounds). At somewhere around two in the morning, this man forced his daughter to don some of his Renaissance gear and have it out. After allegedly fighting for two hours, the girl could no longer stand due to exhaustion, and the fight ended. The incident, however, did not; the sixteen-year-old texted pictures of her injuries to a friend, who called 911. The man was arrested along with the girl's stepmother. The stepmother was charged with failure to intervene.[5]

In one of the accounts I saw (which differed in that the man was said to be the stepfather and the woman the girl's mother), this man thought it was permissible to fight the teenager because she was sixteen. Whether father or stepfather, he apparently did not see the disparity in a three-hundred-pound adult male physically fighting a one-hundred-pound adolescent female. To him, they had a difference of opinion (he thought she was at a crack house, and she said it was just a party), and the way to solve this was to compete in battle, albeit with padding and wooden swords. Of course, given the disparity in age, gender, size, and skill, this was nowhere near a fair fight; it was rigged in the man's favor. This wasn't a fair competition; it was a staged beating, a despicable way for this man to enlarge his horns.

Growing Your Horns

Most men are competitive. We like to push off against something or someone else to make ourselves stronger and to sharpen our skills. We enjoy the thrill of competition. Men have found ways to fight against each other on battlefields since time immemorial. Combat is certainly a high-stakes form of competition. Some men are soldiers, but the majority of us do not actively engage in warfare. Instead, we find other arenas besides a battlefield in which to compete. Some men compete fiercely in the arena of ideas. Others enjoy simulated or mock battles in historical re-creations. Others satisfy that need to compete through any number of sophisticated graphic simulations in video gaming. Others reject the console and choose to compete on a tennis court, a football field, a soccer pitch, a baseball diamond, or a golf course.

In moderation, all of these things are acceptable ways for men to exhibit healthy competition. The problem with the man in Washington was not that he suited up in Renaissance gear; it's that he suited up in Renaissance gear to beat up an adolescent. There is nothing wrong with mock duels and medieval jousting or Civil War battle re-creations. There is nothing wrong with enjoying video games or cheering your hometown sports team. There is nothing wrong with competing against others in sporting contests. There is nothing wrong with any of these things if they stay within the proper parameters of healthy competition. Then they are acceptable horn scraping; they are what men do to test themselves and others, to have fun, be physical, relax, relieve stress, and find ways to bring a sense of thrill into life.

With healthy competition, there is no conflict with values like honesty, integrity, and dependability. Healthy competition allows you to push off the efforts of others, to make yourself stronger, to improve so you can become better. In healthy competition, you do your best to compete against others and learn from those who are better than you. Healthy competition is not about putting anyone else down; it's about using resistance to build you up. This isn't grading yourself on some sort of curve so you can find a way to do the very least and still stay on top. Healthy competition is reaching for excellence and personal best. It's about attaining a higher position and then helping others to get there too.

Competition is healthy when it stays within its proper boundaries and does not venture into the realm of compulsion. It picks its battlefields and its combatants wisely and maturely. It contains the potential for both success and failure. Healthy competition includes honest effort and a fair use of skill. Anything less than honest effort and fair use of skill turns competition into the realm of the unhealthy. Most men want to fight, but they want to fight fair. Unhealthy, mismatched competition is repugnant, and mature men tend to recoil at the thought of contests like the one reported in Washington. That father is not viewed as a hero; he's viewed as a repulsive fool.

We don't root for bullies; we root for the underdog. The bully is considered a coward for starting an unfair fight; though the underdog is smaller and weaker, we applaud him for the courage to compete against the odds. Even if the underdog is defeated, we have more respect for him than the bully. If, somehow, the underdog manages to defeat the bully, we cheer.

In unhealthy competition, the goal is not to find a way for you to be better but to find a way for others to be worse. This type of competition often occurs when men rely too heavily on comparison between themselves and others to gain a sense of self and value. Instead of stretching and growing so you can stand taller, you find a way to undercut the other person. Instead of learning and evaluating so you have a better answer, you lie and misrepresent and undermine what the other person said. Instead of admitting and learning from your own mistakes, you deny and hide them while highlighting the mistakes of others.

Going Offtrack

Competition can be healthy and a very important motivator in a man's life. The challenge is to keep that competitive drive within its proper boundaries. I have found there are a couple of reasons why men go off the healthy track where competition is concerned and begin to veer into the unhealthy side streets of compulsions.

The first reason a man may turn competition into a compulsion is because he develops a reliance on the zing, the sheer physical thrill that happens during competition. There is a physiological reaction that takes place while doing something risky or dangerous. And, for competition to be truly competitive, there needs to be an element of risk and possible danger, even if it's simply getting your pride hurt or getting knocked on your butt. Competing can give you an adrenaline rush that sharpens your focus, quickens your breathing, races your heart, and makes you feel *alive*, with the bigger risk producing the greater rush. You can get this rush running down the field toward the end zone, dodging opposing players, but you can also get it watching the home team score a touchdown. This rush, this zing, is why stadiums across the country fill up with crazed, excited fans, screaming at the top of their lungs. I know the feeling; I love fall football season in Seattle and the zing of thousands of decibel-deafening fans screaming and high-fiving over multiple opposing team false starts.

This competitive zing is also why the casinos in my local area are packed on a Saturday night. It's why Las Vegas and Atlantic City exist, to a great extent. Gambling is voluntary, zing-pursuing risk taking. When you gamble by playing against other people, you get both a monetary win and a personal victory. Even if you're betting against the house, the payoff can be exciting, fueling the desire to do it again, all for the thrill of a big win. That hit—that big win—is one of the key components in the creation of a gambling addiction. Once you've experienced that zing, you keep gambling, longing for another win. The more you gamble to win, the more you generally lose and the greater the compulsion to keep going, to arrive at that one big win that's surely out there for you.

The second reason a man may turn competition into a compulsion is because he sees competition as a way to satisfy a need for dominance. Yes, it's fun and exciting to play, but it can be even more fun and exciting to *win*. For some men, it's not enough just to play the game and let the chips fall where they may. For these men, it's not about the playing; they are obsessed with winning. They want to be the best at everything.

Men who crave dominance will obsessively manipulate circumstances and outcomes in order to win but only in those areas where they place value. Men obsessed with dominance tend to concentrate on black-and-white, winners vs. losers competitions. Obsessive winning is often tied to outward, physical trophies, such as who has the best muscles, the hottest car, the hottest girl, the most money, or most noteworthy accomplishments, also known as "bragging rights." In these dominance contests, the thrill comes not just from winning but also from someone else losing.

These men compete in areas that produce value coming in to them. They rarely will take this dominance competition into areas that produce value going out from them and to other people. For example, dominance competitors do not generally engage in a contest to see who is the most compassionate toward their children or elderly parents or who is the most sacrificial in giving to charities or benevolent outreach. Compassion and sacrifice are too often viewed as subservient behavior.

The so-called "Renaissance man" in the news was not engaged in a fair contest but rather in a display of dominance. The universal response to this story has been one of disgust that would have turned to outrage, I suspect, if the girl's injuries had been severer. We are disgusted by such an egregious example of unfair competition. But, ask yourself, do you put up with smaller, subtler examples of unhealthy competition, either in yourself or in others?

The Cheater

This is the man who, quite simply, cheats. If he's playing a round of golf, he moves the ball or doesn't putt out the green. He lies about his work product, taking credit for the good he doesn't do and refusing to admit responsibility for the bad he does. He is not a man of his word, yet he portrays himself as a man of integrity. He can be extremely verbal and intelligent, but instead of using those talents for the betterment of others, he uses them strictly for betterment of self by being unscrupulously clever. In many ways, his constant cheating is really a game he's playing. If you fail to catch him cheating, well, that's really your fault. Integrity is not something adhered to from the inside but rather something occasionally imposed on him from the outside.

The Constant Competitor

This is the man who constantly competes about seemingly everything. He cannot enjoy a game of golf or tennis, watch a baseball or football game, without engaging in some sort of bet with the people around him. He'll wager on inconsequential things, like how long it takes for the elevator to arrive at his floor. If he wins, it's pay up. If he loses, it's double or nothing on whatever comes next to mind. When insisting upon competing, he'll say things like "just to make it fun" or "to sweeten the pot." With this man, there are no time-outs and the game is never over. He's playing the odds that if he keeps at it long enough, he'll either win at the next random wager or you'll get tired of the whole thing and just move on. His constant badgering is a form of horn-scraping.

The Backstabber

This is the man who engages in all-out competition but never out in the open. Instead, he maneuvers behind your back, looking for advantages, sniffing out weaknesses, planning the best time for him and the worst time for you to strike. Instead of meeting you head-to-head, he works in the shadows through innuendo, whispers, flattery, and gossip. If confronted with his slimy behavior, he'll deny it and claim it's all a misunderstanding—on your part, of course. This man is always engaged in battle because he considers everyone around him to be an enemy. He has no allegiance, no loyalty, except to himself.

135

These three unhealthy competitors are often found among men in the business world because business and work are major competitive arenas for men. We derive a great deal of sense of self and worth from what we do and how we're perceived within that venue, as we've talked about before. Men who would never consider using one of these methods to gain the upper hand on the athletic fields of youth can sometimes compromise those principles when it's money in the bank instead of points on the board.

Taking Charge

Most men like competition when it's straightforward and honest. We don't mind going head-to-head against someone if it's a fair fight. We don't like to be bait-and-switched; we don't like to be cheated or lied to; we don't like to be hit low or hit late. At least, that's how we want to be treated. It gets a little trickier on the other side of that Golden Rule thing. It's hard for us to give up an advantage, even if that advantage is not found by taking the high road. We have reasons and excuses and rationales to justify our own unfair and unhealthy means of competing. Think about what you'd do in the following situations.

Scenario #1

The boss calls you into his office to talk to you about a work situation. It appears a co-worker in your department has made an error in reporting important information under the new accounting system. Your boss wants to talk to you about it, to determine if it's unintentional or if there's something more to it. Times are tight and the firm is experiencing a 20 percent loss in revenues, so you know everyone's work product is being watched. You know you're in competition with this co-worker for your job if cuts are made. While you weren't aware of your co-worker's mistake, you realize you made the exact same mistake the week earlier. Sure, you fixed it before anyone noticed, but you didn't tell anyone about the mistake and alert either your co-workers or your supervisor to this potential problem with the new system. What do you tell your boss about your co-worker? What do you tell your boss about yourself?

Scenario #2

Your sixteen-year-old comes to you and wants your help getting a car. You tell him he can have his own car if he gets his grades up. When he asks what that means, you tell him he needs to pull between a 3.75 and a 4.0 grade point average for two consecutive quarters at school in order for you to consider him worthy enough to get his own car. This is a kid who has been a solid B student for his entire schooling. He's gotten a couple of As, but he's also pulled in Cs. He works hard to maintain that B average. You've thrown down the gauntlet for a significant increase in his GPA. Is this fair?

Scenario #3

You're out hitting the pavement, trying to drum up sales. You go into a new business to try to talk to the owner, only to find your competitor from another company has beat you in the door. There's his card on the counter. You pick up the card and ask the owner about it. He tells you about that guy coming in and then asks what you know about him. The owner says he's heard this guy has had three jobs in the past five years and has a lousy reputation among the local merchants. You realize the owner has gotten this guy and someone else with a similar name mixed up. You're familiar with both of them, and the guy who beat you in the door is a pretty stand-up guy. What do you say to the owner?

Scenario #4

You're sitting on the couch, watching your team lose its third straight game. Your teenage daughter comes into the room and starts toward the kitchen. You ask her if she'll put a bag of popcorn into the microwave for you. She explains she's already late to get to a friend's house and doesn't have time. You start to question her about where she's going and why. You ask her if her homework is done and if all of her chores are finished. She gets upset at your questioning and you get upset at her attitude. You end up telling her she can't go after all and she'd better do something about her back talking. Was your decision a fair one?

These scenarios may not be exactly like ones you've had to deal with in your own life, but I'm hopeful they will contain enough similarities so that you can put yourself within each one and determine what you'd do. If you need to, read them over again and answer honestly. Write down the answers if you want, but make sure to use each of these scenarios to help identify just where you've drawn your own personal lines of fairness in each situation.

Here is how I answer each of them:

Scenario #1

Even though I wouldn't be happy about doing it, I'd tell the truth about my own mistake. I'd explain that, though I fixed it on my own and didn't bring it up at the time, it appears there may be a glitch in the software or in training, because both of us made the same mistake. Instead of dwelling on my co-worker, I'd give my boss the information and let him draw his own conclusions without going out of my way to make my co-worker look bad. If someone has to be let go, it's probably going to be on general work productivity and not on this one problem. If I do my job to the best of my ability, that's fighting fair.

Scenario #2

A fair competition means that both parties have a shot at victory. This one is not fair and will only cause my teenager frustration. If he's been doing his best and that best is hovering around a 3.0, asking him to jump almost a full grade point isn't realistic. Setting such a high bar is going to make him feel like a failure—or he could become suspicious that I set the bar so high because I knew he couldn't reach it and don't really want him to have a car in the first place. A teenage son's first car should be a bonding time for father and son, not a setup for a fractured relationship. Setting the bar at an achievable goal is fair.

Scenario #3

It's tempting to just plead ignorance and allow the owner to keep the wrong impression of my competition. Tempting, but that's really the coward's way out. I know it isn't true and need to say so first thing. After clearing the air, I can then shift the conversation to me and my company, what I can do for him and the advantages I bring to the table. Hopefully, because I was up-front and honest about my competition, this business owner will realize I'm a man of honesty and integrity. That's fighting fair.

Scenario #4

Getting into a fight with my teenage daughter because I'm mad about my team losing is ridiculous. It's also, unfortunately, what parents do sometimes to make ourselves feel better. In this scenario, getting angry at something I can control—my teenager—compensates for getting angry at something I can't control—whether my team is going to win. This fight wasn't about popcorn or where she was going or homework or whatever. I was looking for an easy smackdown, and she just happened to walk in the room. It could have been another family member or the dog, for that matter.

Did I "win" and exercise my parental authority? Yes, but if I keep fighting unfairly like this, I'm going to lose my relationship with my daughter.

Again, hopefully these scenarios have helped you think about your own life situations, decisions, and values. Often, these situations of unfair fighting haunt men, either because they were the ones who were fought against unfairly or because they were unfair themselves and have trouble forgiving themselves for their behavior.

I really appreciate the comprehensive approach to "unfairness" represented in the Twelve Steps of Alcoholics Anonymous, including being honest about where, how, and who you've wronged and taking intentional steps to make amends. There is just something about writing out the times, places, and people impacted by your "unfairness." In that spirit, I'd like you to write out two personal situations. If you're not big on words, draw a picture or create a symbol for each of these moments of unfairness in your life.

For the first one, I'd like you to choose a time when you were unfair to someone else. For the second one, I'd like you to choose a time when someone was unfair to you. What can you learn about yourself, the other person, and life in general through these situations? If you had each to do over again, what would you do differently?

You can look at life as one big competition—you against other people, you against the world, your older self now against your younger self then—through all sorts of lenses and comparisons. When you think of life as a competition, other people become either your allies or your adversaries. After all, every other person you come into contact with will have their own opinions, wants, desires, preferences, goals, and outcomes. In this life competition, when those goals mesh with yours, you're allies. When they don't, you are adversaries, and your predominant viewpoint is a black-and-white scenario of if-I-win-you-lose-if-you-win-I-lose. From this viewpoint, conversations become arguments, differences of opinion become dividing lines. Opposition becomes personal. This is a toxic atmosphere, and other people, people you love and care about, may withdraw from you and your incessant competition.

Your role as a man is not to prove to everyone how strong you are or how right you are, how big you are or how lucky you are. When you insist on teaching those lessons through unhealthy and unfair competition, you hammer home by necessity the inverse as well—how weak they are, how wrong they are, how small they are, how unlucky they are. These are not lessons most people want to hear. At some point, they will reject you and your lessons. The tearing down of other people should not be the goal of your battles.

Men are supposed to be knights in shining armor, rescuing the weak, righting wrongs, and fighting for justice. There is something viscerally wrong with armored knights hacking through a crowd of defenseless peasants. When you engage in unfair, unhealthy competition, you end up the equivalent of that three-hundred-pound man beating up his one-hundred-pound daughter. You are not a competitor, you are a bully. Bullies may end up winning the battle, but they seldom end up winning the war.

In this troubled, turbulent world we live in, we need competitors. We need men who are willing to take the hits and fight fairly, even when others do not. We need men who understand the value example of healthy competition they provide to those around them. Other men need to see and learn from your healthy example. Boys, who will be men someday, need to learn from your healthy example. You need to benefit from your own healthy example, to keep the temptation of unhealthy competition at bay.

Men have gotten a bad rap over the years by taking advantage of other people and engaging in unfair competition against those weaker or at a disadvantage. It's time to turn that around and return the male competitive drive to a positive, empowering, even noble pursuit. We may be in the twenty-first century, but I don't think we'll ever get over the need for men as knights in shining armor.

Reaching Higher

There is nothing wrong with healthy competition. After all, Hebrews 10:24 tells us we should spur one another on to love and good deeds. Healthy, fair competition brings out the best in both parties, allowing excellence to prevail. Unhealthy, unfair competition isn't interested in excellence or integrity or the best outcome. Unhealthy, unfair competition is interested in winning. That is not how God's people should act.

> The world is unprincipled. It's dog-eat-dog out there! The world doesn't fight fair. But we don't live or fight our battles that way—never have and never will. The tools of our trade aren't for marketing or manipulation, but they are for demolishing that entire massively corrupt culture. We use our powerful God-tools for smashing warped philosophies, tearing down barriers erected against the truth of God, fitting every loose thought and emotion and impulse into the structure of life shaped by Christ. Our tools are ready at hand for clearing the ground of every obstruction and building lives of obedience into maturity.
>
> 2 Corinthians 10:3–6 MSG

Our thoughts and emotions and impulses must be shaped by Christ. Christ is not a three-hundred-pound bully beating up a one-hundred-pound teenager. Christ isn't constantly wagering with us in order to watch us lose, time and time again. God is on our side and has stacked the deck in our favor. Christ doesn't say one thing to our face and do something else behind our back. God does not compete against us; God contends for us.

9

Consumption

I never worried about what I ate," he assured me, clearly defensive. "When I was younger, I ate and drank what I wanted. I never worried about it." By the look on his face and the fact he'd mentioned the word *worried* twice in practically the same sentence, I knew that might have been true in the past but it wasn't true now. He was worried; he just didn't want to admit it. His marriage was in trouble, his business was stressful, and he was about eighty pounds overweight—he had reason to be worried.

The thought of dieting, of being worried about his weight, however, seemed pushed into some sort of female corner. Big guys weren't supposed to care about their waistlines; only preoccupied, narcissistic women did that. Yeah, he could take off the weight. He had before, plenty of times, but of course, that was when he was younger. He'd just been too busy lately with other stuff to pay much attention. He'd get to his weight when he was ready.

He let me know he resented the whole subject. He'd come in for stress issues, not weight-loss advice. He resented what he'd been told by the dietitian and took offense when she'd recommended he lay off white bread and Dr Pepper. What was wrong with white bread, he wanted to know, and he'd been drinking Dr Pepper without a problem for years. Frustrated, he told me that with so much going haywire in his life, ordering at a restaurant was about the only time he actually got what he wanted.

I've found that women often cope with their size by constantly thinking about their weight issues. Men, however, often do the opposite; they cope with their size by constantly dismissing their weight issues. Women can live from mirror to mirror, obsessed with what they see. Men can live without mirrors at all, blinded by what they don't see.

I'll admit I had trouble figuring out what to call this chapter. I decided on "Consumption" for a couple of reasons. One reason is most of us men don't tend to connect with anything smacking of the word *diet* and certainly not anything to do with an eating disorder. That's female stuff to most guys. So a chapter called "food" or "dieting" or "disordered eating" would present a barrier. Consumption, however, is not a term that's been feminized. After all, you *consume* food; you *consume* alcohol. It's a much more generic term. It doesn't trigger any mental pictures of waif-thin anorexics or weight-obsessed females.

I also chose consumption because of an older definition of the word. Consumption used to be the word for tuberculosis and had a meaning of the body wasting away, with life and vitality consumed by the condition. Think of the last Western you saw on the fight at the OK Corral. Doc Holliday was said to have died from consumption. As strange as it may seem, I've known men today who have also died from "consumption"—not the tuberculosis kind but from overconsumption. The decisions they made about what they consumed, what they ate and drank, day after day, year after year, caused their health and vitality to waste away prematurely. The statistics can be harsh. Food and weight issues aren't just for women; men ignore them at their own peril.

What Used to Work Doesn't Anymore

Getting older can be really irritating. Your metabolism shifts around, your life responsibilities change, and your body no longer tolerates what it used to. When you were younger and picked up some extra weight, you'd just cut back for a few weeks, add an extra pickup game of basketball, and before you knew it, your jeans were fitting fine again. You could run more and play more and work out more, and that was just fine because you set your own schedule. You bounced back physically, and little aches and pains were little because of the amount of time they lasted, not because of how much they bugged you on a daily basis. Back then, all your tried-and-true strategies for getting into shape or staying within a certain weight worked like a charm. You could consume what you wanted with marginal consequence because your body was a lean-muscled, testosterone-fueled engine, burning off all those extra calories and burning up those minor and sometimes major consumption indiscretions. Of course, that was before you got older and got married and had kids and started working all the time and sitting all the time and worrying all the time. Like I said, aging can be irritating.

Many men equate weight gain with age. It's different for women. Many women don't equate weight gain with a specific age because they've always felt fat. For many women, fear of weight gain has been a constant companion, an ever-present albatross, since adolescence.

Because men don't tend to worry as much about their weight during adolescence and young adulthood, those weight fears often don't show up until later in life. When they're younger, weight isn't considered a problem. But in their thirties and forties, they're slowly ambushed by incremental weight gain. They may notice tipping out on the scales a bit higher but aren't as quick as women to push the panic button. They're busy working on families and careers, so what's a couple of pounds here and there? Besides, getting fat is what happens to you when you get older.

By the time these men get into their fifties and actually stop long enough to really look at themselves and their weight, they think, *Whoa, when did that happen?* They'll try what they used to do in order to drop weight and quickly realize those things don't work anymore. For one, it's a lot harder to give up Dr Pepper or Samuel Adams or Jack Daniels after forty-plus years of deep devotion. It's a lot harder to run, *period*, let alone run the weight off, when you're older and larger than you've ever been. You're more tired than you've ever been, sorer than you've ever dreamed of, and more discouraged than you've ever felt. The path of least resistance is to continue to eat your nachos while you sit in the evening and critique what other men do on ESPN.

Don't Call Me Late for Dinner

There was a time when you could play or run or bike or skateboard all day long. Having to stop for lunch or dinner was a bother. Food was secondary, and eating was something you did to keep doing something else. You ate your broccoli and drank your milk and only had two cookies because your mom was watching out for you and it was the only way to be released from the table so you could go play. Back then, because your mom was watching out for your nutritional needs, food was actually in its proper place. Food was nutrition to fuel your day and your play. It was part of your life but wasn't a lifestyle choice. That happened later on as you grew older.

One of the first things teenagers realize is that they have a great deal of freedom over what they eat. Pizza for breakfast is a rite of passage. So is downing multiple cans of soda or power drinks per day. As long as you find a way to pay for it, you can have it. No more meal monitors telling you what you should and shouldn't eat or drink. Consuming what you want, when you want, and in the quantity you want is one of those perks of adulthood. When you're young and newly released to the equivalent of a never-ending culinary Mardi Gras, the long-term effects of such consumption are relegated to the obscure fine print. You'll read it later. As a maturing adult, you end up reading that fine print on digital bathroom scales and on lab reports, on pharmaceutical disclosures and in doctor's notations.

When you were younger, you resented when meals interrupted life. As you get older, you may find you resent when life interrupts meals, especially if the number of pleasures in your life has dwindled along with your energy level and drive. With so many aspects of life out of your control, a good meal and a nice glass of whatever can become a much-anticipated reward and end-of-day ritual. You know what you like and what you've come to rely on to soothe the stress of the day, to reward your effort and hard work, to provide that reliable sense of relief. Consuming food and drink subtly moves from something that fuels you nutritionally to something that fills you emotionally.

Disordered Eating

Okay, I'm now going to use the term "disordered eating." That's what happens when food and drink move out of the Nutrition

Box and into the Emotions Box. When food and drink stay within the Nutrition Box, it's possible for that box to be filled. There is a fill line at the top of the Nutrition Box that says "Enough." The Emotions Box has no such fill line. On the contrary, there's a false bottom in that box so it never stays full. You can just keep pouring food and drink down that box and it's not going to be enough; all of that consumption is going into the wrong box. Your boxes have gotten out of order or *disordered*.

Emotional eating is not the sole property of women; men do it too. Men come to rely on food, just like women do, to eat the hurts away, to salve the wounds and make the world disappear, if only for a little while. Men overeat and drink too much and put on excess weight. All this extra weight makes it harder to move and be active. The less you move and are active, the easier it is to gain even more weight. The body increases in fat and loses muscle. Testosterone ratios drop, and muscles become flaccid and shrink. This is the male terror associated with aging—this loss of youthful, masculine vigor. When the terror becomes too overwhelming, it's just easier to pretend it doesn't exist, avoid the mirrors, and put off changes until a later date.

Just One More

No chapter on eating or drinking or consumption, or whatever you want to call it, would be complete without talking about the consumption of alcohol. If you're one of those men who can drink in moderation and keep it within proper boundaries, congratulations. As a licensed chemical dependency professional, I'm all too familiar with the devastation—personal, familial, financial, professional, and physical—that an alcohol addiction can create in a man's life. There are certain men, of course, who can take alcohol or leave it, but there are others who need to stay as far away from it as possible because of the havoc it has caused in their lives. Between those two polar ends are a great deal of men who need to keep a constant eye on what they drink, when they drink, why they drink, and how much they drink.

Too many of those men in the middle derive a sort of pride in what they consider their ability to hold their liquor. They may not drink every day or even every week, but drinking is viewed as a competitive sport, with the winner designated as whoever is left standing. Consuming alcohol is not a skill to be honed and brandished in competition against others. The only way you can acclimate your physical body to tolerate more alcohol is to drink it. The more you drink, the more your body adapts. The more your body adapts, the more alcohol it needs to function. Becoming adept at alcohol consumption doesn't win you the prize; it makes you an alcoholic.

There are too many men in the middle who start out drinking in moderation, but then something happens. They go through a tough time at work or at home. That mug of beer or that glass of wine in the evening helps get them over the rough spots. Even after the circumstance is over, the drinking continues. It's not much, just a glass or two, but those one or two merge into just one more and keep on going night after night. Eventually, the first thing they touch in the evening when they get home isn't their wife or their dog, it's their drink. Sometimes they wonder if it's getting out of hand, but they know they can stop anytime they want to; they just don't want to, and it's not like they're getting drunk or anything.

Many of these men believe that alcohol is synonymous with a good time. They can't go out to dinner with friends, go to a sporting event, take an overnight trip, or do just about anything without having a six-pack or longnecked bottle somewhere in reserve. They need the alcohol to relax, unwind, and really enjoy the evening or the event. If alcohol is missing, it's seen as a detriment, as a negative on an otherwise positive day.

Often these men are as oblivious to and in denial of the amount of alcohol they consume as they are to the amount and type of food they consume. Alcohol is just so much a part of the fabric of their lives, they really don't pay attention to how much they're drinking, why they're drinking, how they feel when they drink, and how they feel when they don't. Because of this, it can be difficult to step back and evaluate the consequences of their alcohol use.

The National Institutes of Alcohol Abuse and Alcoholism has a short way to help identify if alcohol has become an issue. It's called the CAGE and has four basic questions:

C Have you ever felt you should **cut down** on your drinking?

A Have people **annoyed** you by criticizing your drinking?

G Have you ever felt bad or **guilty** about your drinking?

E **Eye opener:** Have you ever had a drink first thing in the morning to steady your nerves or to get rid of a hangover?

According to NIAAA, "Two positive responses are considered a positive test and indicate further assessment is warranted."[6]

If you answered yes to two of those four questions, it's not time to take the test over and find a way to answer yes to only one so you won't have to do anything about it. If you answered yes to two or more of those four questions, it's time to get an alcohol assessment done by a professional chemical dependency counselor or whoever is licensed to do substance assessments where you live. This isn't going away, and it's not something you can do on your own. Alcohol creates dependence, both physical and emotional.

Don't mess around with it; get tested, find out where you're really at, and get the help you need.

Taking Charge

Consumption doesn't have to be a word that only comes after "over." It is possible to reclaim consumption for the Nutrition Box and clear food and drink out of the bottomless-pit Emotions Box. (You might also consider that the Emotions Box is a bottomless pit *only* when you try to fill it up with something other than emotions, like food and drink.) Getting a handle on overconsumption is certainly something to try on your own (unless what you're overconsuming is alcohol, and then refer to the above section about getting professional help). If you're overconsuming Dr Pepper and not Jack Daniels, there's plenty of material out there about how to eat and drink more healthily. It's not like you're oblivious to some of the choices you're making. You know two or three things you could do, today, that would have a positive impact on your health.

It may be you've just been ignoring what you're doing, avoiding the mirrors and those health impacts because, if all things were equal, you'd really like to just keep doing what you're doing. It may be you're still young enough to compensate for the overindulgences without overt consequences. In either case, time is not on your side. The only way to turn this thing around is to be up-front about where you're at and determine what you need to do to move forward toward better health.

So, in order for you to begin to really recognize your eating and drinking patterns, I want you to envision two boxes—a Nutrition Box and an Emotions Box. These are the only two boxes you can use. Every drink you take, every bite you put in your mouth must go in one box or the other. You can do this in your head, but I'd rather you kept some sort of log. It can be as simple as one sheet of paper that says "Nutrition Box" and another sheet of paper that says "Emotions Box."

Over the course of the next week, or longer if you can keep it up, either mark in your mind or mark down on your log everything you eat or drink in either box. At the end of a week, take a look at how much of your consumption is going into the Nutrition Box and how much of your consumption is dedicated to the Emotions Box. One way to know if something is supposed to go into the Emotions Box is if you know you really shouldn't be eating that or eating that much but are just going to do it anyway. Defiant (*I'll eat whatever I want*), angry (*Don't tell me what I can or can't eat*) consuming is going right into that Emotions Box.

Then, over the next week, start to make one daily change that moves a food or drink choice from the Emotions Box to the Nutrition Box. Make sure to mark the change. Work on that change for a week and then add another the following week.

Knowledge is power. Understanding what you're doing can be the first step toward change. Believe me, I know how hard it is to make dietary changes. Sometimes, understanding what you need to do can give you the motivation to make those changes. Oftentimes, however, more help is needed. There are reasons why that Emotions Box is getting so many of your consumption choices. You may find you experience resistance to moving more of your choices back into the Nutrition Box. If so, I encourage you to seek out helpful resources. I have found tremendous value in combining medical, nutritional information with counseling and therapeutic support for healthy life-style changes. After all, if this were just a matter of knowledge alone, there would be vastly more people on the Nutrition side of things.

That Emotions Box is powerful and can have an almost gravitational pull on your consumption choices. If that's the case with you, don't hesitate to call in reinforcements. The choice of whom you call is still yours. Getting professional help for eating is not a female thing, it's a taking-back-control thing. It's your life and your health and your future. You've got things to do, and you need to be strong and healthy to do them.

Reaching Higher

Because you are a spiritual being, you will experience spiritual hunger when your spiritual needs are not met. This isn't a truth I can quantify or graph or produce black-and-white data for. Spiritual things are much more ephemeral, as John reminds us in John 3:8. The Spirit is like the wind. You can't see the wind, but you can still see the effects of the wind. In the same way, you cannot see spiritual hunger, but you can see the effects of spiritual hunger. I see it in my practice all the time.

When people are spiritually hungry, they often turn to physical food in an attempt to fill the void. A relationship with food is substituted for a relationship with God. Food provides the reassurance, the comfort, the companionship, and in some cases, the love, instead of God. The greater the spiritual hunger, the more food and drink can be used to compensate. There is an amazing parallel in the devotion some people will give to their food or drink of choice. It is an almost religious devotion, complete with a type of "faith" in the substance's ability to make everything right.

This type of devotion has been seen before. It is idol worship, turning an inanimate object into an object of worship, devotion, and adoration. Back in more primitive cultures, they used objects of stone and wood and gold. Nowadays, we use objects of bread and sugar and alcohol.

Man-made idols don't work (from Isa. 44):

The blacksmith takes a tool
 and works with it in the coals;
he shapes an idol with hammers,
 he forges it with the might of his arm.
He gets hungry and loses his strength;
 he drinks no water and grows faint.

The carpenter measures with a line
 and makes an outline with a marker;
he roughs it out with chisels
 and marks it with compasses.
He shapes it in the form of man,
 of man in all his glory,
  that it may dwell in a shrine.

He cut down cedars,
 or perhaps took a cypress or oak.
He let it grow among the trees of the forest,
 or planted a pine, and the rain made it grow.

It is man's fuel for burning;
 some of it he takes and warms himself,
 he kindles a fire and bakes bread.
But he also fashions a god and worships it;
 he makes an idol and bows down to it.

Half of the wood he burns in the fire;
 over it he prepares his meal,
 he roasts his meat and eats his fill.
He also warms himself and says,
 "Ah! I am warm; I see the fire."

From the rest he makes a god, his idol;
 he bows down to it and worships.
He prays to it and says,
 "Save me; you are my god."

They know nothing, they understand nothing;
>   their eyes are plastered over so they cannot see,
>   and their minds closed so they cannot understand.

No one stops to think,
>   no one has the knowledge or understanding to say,
"Half of it I used for fuel;
>   I even baked bread over its coals,
>   I roasted meat and I ate.
Shall I make a detestable thing from what is left?
>   Shall I bow down to a block of wood?"

He feeds on ashes, a deluded heart misleads him;
>   he cannot save himself, or say,
>   "Is not this thing in my right hand a lie?"

That beer in your hand is a lie. That fork in your hand is a lie. The desire to worship, to express adoration, to receive comfort and assurance is spiritual and can be filled only through a relationship with God. People have always attempted to substitute things they can control for a God who is bigger than self. They have always attempted to substitute things they create for the One who created them. It's never worked and just leaves the spiritual void unfilled, open and raw.

God continually told the Israelites to put down their useless idols and turn their devotion to him. The stuff we use for idols has changed over the years, but God's desire to fill up every void of our souls hasn't.

PART 2

THE WHY

10

Fear of Who You're Not

I look in the mirror, and it's never enough." Normally you might think that sort of statement would come from a woman speaking about her physical appearance, but this time it came from Ted, a very successful businessman. The "never enough" had nothing to do with a dissatisfaction over his outside and everything to do with a dissatisfaction over his inside.

A woman will often strive to achieve that one elusive moment in time when all the stars align and she attains her dreamed-of vision of physical perfection. I have watched women give up incredibly valuable things in life, including, tragically, life itself, reaching toward that outward goal. This striving runs as background noise in her life, creating an omnipresent static of dissatisfaction.

I've also watched men give up incredibly valuable things in life, reaching toward a similar, elusive vision. However, this male vision is generally not centered on the physical; instead, it is centered on an inward vision of self, of manhood. Both sexes will develop a sort of tunnel vision, a hyperfocus on the goal just out of reach.

161

This vision is so compelling that both will fail to pay attention to the here and now, to the people and things around them, jettisoning whatever is necessary to get one step closer to the prize.

For Ted, the prize was approval from his father. The tragedy was that Ted's father had developed Alzheimer's and was no longer capable of recognizing his son, let alone recognizing his son's achievements. That did not deter Ted, however, from continually trying.

His father grew up a natural academic, becoming an engineer with an advanced degree, and spent his working life with charts and measurements, quantifiable tasks and outcomes. Production was how he defined success. Ted, however, was not a natural at books; he was a natural at people. Rejecting college after a disastrous first year, he became a salesman for a vitamin company. Ted was a great salesman. If he wanted to, he could have made money selling ice in Alaska. Financially, he was very successful, but the real prize he sought—his father's approval—was always elusive.

"I didn't take the path Dad wanted, and he never forgave me," Ted explained, already using the past tense when speaking of his father.

"But couldn't he at least appreciate your success and how you've been able to take care of your family?" I asked, trying to find some measure of approval Ted could grab on to.

"No," he said bluntly. "He always thought my job was a scam. The more successful I became, the more annoyed he got and the more he kept saying I was just ripping people off on useless products. He said that wasn't the way a decent man made a living.

"I just . . ." He stopped and collected himself. "I wanted him to just once tell me he was proud of me. Now it's too late. I've flat run out of time."

My friend Cynthia Rowland once described the motivation behind her eating disorder as feeling like she was "damaged goods."

That metaphor has always stayed with me because of how significant it was in Cynthia's life and struggle and because of how prevalent that same theme is over and over again with so many women. In some ways, Ted felt the same way, like "damaged goods." His father made it clear that he was ashamed of Ted, of his choices in life and how he made a living. Because of this, Ted considered himself deficient, defective, no matter how successful he became, because he consistently failed to measure up to his father's expectations.

His father saw life and manhood as concretely as a set of engineering charts. He had in his mind a template for success as a person and as a man, and his son's choices and even attributes did not conform to the pattern. Because the manner of his son's success was suspect, no amount of success could overcome that approval barrier. It was a hurdle too high.

High Hurdles

A friend of mine ran track in high school. He was pretty amazing, and I always enjoyed watching him run. Not only did he run sprints but he also ran the high hurdles. As if running fast wasn't enough, in the hurdles he had to stride airborne over a series of obstacles. That's what Ted had been doing his whole life. He was an incredibly fast runner—a great salesman—and able to win races in business. What tripped him up were the hurdles to personal value and worth that his father's actions, attitudes, and opinions had placed in his way. It didn't matter how many other races in life he won, Ted couldn't consider himself a success because he kept getting tripped up by those high hurdles.

As men, we do not like to be found inadequate. Rather, we will do just about anything to be viewed as strong, effective, competent, and necessary. In his father's eyes, Ted struck out on all four.

- Ted was not strong, because he had chosen the "easy" way out through business and avoided the "challenging" path of academic success.
- Ted was not effective, because his work didn't produce anything of "real value" but only monetary success.
- Yes, Ted was competent, but in a dishonorable way by "tricking" people to buy a "useless" product.
- A relationship with Ted became extraneous to his father because Ted's chosen pursuits in life were in such contradiction to what his father found valuable and worthwhile.

Because of Ted's supposed deficiencies, his father had never shown respect to him as a man.

Fear Less

So much of the male psyche is tied to competition. There is the thrill of the challenge, the thrill of dominance, the thrill of cause and effect. We want to make a difference, in our work and in the lives of the people around us. We want to be seen as part of a team, but we also want to be acknowledged and respected for what we uniquely contribute to that team.

The first team we're a part of is our family. There is certainly a larger, full family team, but there is also a smaller, gender-specific family team. A father and son constitute a powerful team. Once a small boy grasps the concept of gender, he aligns himself with his father, looking to his father for approval, acceptance, guidance, and respect. One of the most profound tragedies of this current age is that so many boys are separated or estranged from their fathers. An essential component of manhood is lost when fathers do not know how to be in relationship with their sons. A breakdown in that first father-son team creates a deep well of sadness in men that frequently proves immune to time, distance, and even death.

There is a second teaming that occurs within the father-son relationship that is pivotal. The first teaming happens during childhood and is based on maleness. The second teaming happens during late adolescence/early adulthood and is based on manhood. There is an important developmental pivot point when a father acknowledges his son as a man—not just as a male but as a man, with all of the shadings of honor, integrity, respect, and responsibility that word infers.

Ripe within this rite of passage, this acknowledgment of manhood, is the sense of potential and the gift of future. When a son knows and understands that his father believes in him, is proud of him, has confidence in him, and loves him, it sets the foundation for the son's adult life going forward. It is vital that a boy sees himself as a man through his father's eyes. When this doesn't happen, the son grows up to be a man in constant search of that withheld vision. Seeds of doubt are hurled upon the boy's soul, seeds that can grow over time into full-fledged fears, casting shadows far into the future.

Fear is a primal response. It is overwhelming and altering. Fear hijacks reason. It shifts the personal landscape and reorders priorities. Fear lies at the heart, I believe, of many of the battles men face. The combatant may be pornography or substance abuse, anger or promiscuity, isolation or escape, underachieving or overworking, competing, consuming, or lying, but the real puppet master behind them all, pulling the strings on compulsive behaviors, is fear.

Ted already knew he was less than the man his father had wanted him to be. Why didn't Ted just dismiss his dad, brush off his opinions as old-fashioned and outdated, and live his life the way he wanted without regret? First, he loved his dad, and as painful as it was, his father's opinion mattered to him. Second, a part of Ted lived in fear that his dad's judgment on his life and choices—essentially on his manhood—were somehow, even just marginally, correct.

Ted was afraid he really wasn't strong. He conceded he could have done better in school but chose not to. He admitted he regretted not trying harder and at least going a little farther in school. Looking back over his life, he realized he often looked for and chose the easiest way he could find out of challenges, which for him was talking other people into solving his challenges for him.

Ted was afraid he wouldn't be effective in another line of work. He'd kind of fallen into the one he was in. He expressed some surprise at how successful he was. Over the years, he'd thought about doing something else but was terrified his success was a fluke and his dad would be proved right if he tried and failed at a different job. So, even though he didn't always like his job and occasionally dreamed of doing something else, fear kept him firmly locked into position.

Ted knew he was competent—his paycheck verified that. But he was always fearful of how others, including his father, viewed what he did. After all, it wasn't a brick-and-mortar business but relied more on down lines and multiple marketing platforms. People still tended to look at him funny when they found out what he did for a living. He'd heard more jokes than he wanted to count about how you should never accept a dinner invitation from Ted.

Ted was afraid of not being needed. He'd already seen that happen in his own life as he watched his father's love and affection skip over him to land on the grandkids. There were times he worried about what his affluence was doing to his relationship with his family. Having money was definitely a perk, but did his family really love him or did they love what he could give them? He wanted to make a difference in the lives of his family but was afraid the only difference he'd made was a monetary one.

All of these fears combined to undermine the respect Ted had for himself as a man, as a businessman, as a husband, and as a father. Monetary successes and business accolades were a pale substitute for the respect he craved from his father. In the back of his mind, he viewed his success as a temporary thing, a serendipitous house of cards, something that could collapse at any time. This line of thinking brought on a new round of fears as he worried about what he would do and how he would handle it if the one bucket he'd placed all his self-worth into—the bucket of business success—suddenly started leaking. Who would he be? What would he have left? What would he lose?

Filling the Voids

Fears create black holes of negativity that capture bright spots in life, inexorably sucking these positives into it. The bigger the fears become, the greater their centrifugal force and the more bright spots you need to replace the ones that get swallowed up. That's where compulsive behaviors can come into play as you try to create more and more bright spots in life to outrun the rate at which they are extinguished by fear. When this happens, the compulsion becomes not the activity itself but the need for the activity to keep the fear and the darkness at bay. Compulsive behaviors thrive in an environment of fear-based manhood.

Fear is uncomfortable and comes with very uncomfortable companions like anger, guilt, and shame. Living with these unwelcome companions produces even more discomfort, like anxiety, worry, and stress. Adulthood wasn't sold to you as an uncomfortable time. It was billed as a time of being in charge and in control, a time when you created your own comfort and nobody could tell you differently.

The bad news, the discomfort part, of adulthood comes as a bit of a shock, but fortunately there is a "good news" component. Is it harder than you thought to be an adult? Yes, but the "good news" is, there is a whole array of behaviors and activities you can engage in as an adult to take the sting out of that discomfort. The activities we've talked about in this book are frequently used by men to take the sting out of discomfort. It would be useless to argue that many of them aren't pleasurable; they are. They produce a numbing effect that removes the pain for a time. They numb the pain but they don't do anything to remove the source of the pain. It's like having a toothache and day after day, month after month, year after year, using only a topical gel to numb it. At some point, the only logical course to deal with the pain is to deal with the tooth.

Taking Charge

Ted experienced fears in his life due to the rejection by his father. Maybe that's something you can relate to and maybe it's not. Perhaps you've been rejected by another family member or close friend. Maybe you've felt rejected by other men in general. Whatever the source of your fear, it's time for you to put down the gel (the remote, the computer, the sex, the wallet, the food, or the "whatever" it is that numbs your pain) and deal with the tooth.

In order to be healthy, every man must come face-to-face with his own inadequacies. That can be difficult to do when you're so busy pretending they don't exist or frantically keeping yourself so busy you won't notice them. You need to stop moving, stop numbing, stop denying long enough to really look at what they are. Warning: doing this is uncomfortable. You'll need to accept the discomfort—take that trip to the dentist—and find out which tooth is causing all the problems.

Ideally, I'd like for you to do this next exercise in actuality instead of in your head. You'll need access to either a garbage disposal or a paper shredder. What I'd like you to do is write down all of the positive things in your life that you feel you're missing out on because of your behaviors, actions, and attitudes.

Here's how to do this if you're going to use a garbage disposal. The garbage disposal represents your black holes of fear and negativity. I want you to name it. It could be pornography, alcohol, working too much, isolating too much—whatever you've identified as your particular battle or battles.

Next, write down all the positives in your life that are getting sucked into that black hole of negativity. It could be health, family relationships, or intimacy. Really take the time to identify all the things being negatively affected by your black hole/garbage disposal. Take an apple and cut it into the number of positives you're missing out on. If you have five, cut the apple into five sections; if you have eight, cut the apple into eight. You get the picture.

Run the water, which represents the minutes, hours, and days you're wasting to keep that black hole/garbage disposal working. Then, naming each positive thing, send each piece of apple down the drain to be ground up and pulverized by your black hole. (Enough of a visual for you?)

You can also do this with a paper shredder, though, personally, I'm partial to the garbage disposal for sheer effect. If you're going to use the paper shredder, label it with the name of your negative. Then, write all of the positives being destroyed by that negative on separate sheets of paper. Turn on the shredder, and one by one obliterate the joys in your life.

As stark as this exercise is, that's what's happening to your life, your joys, your relationships, and your health. By using your habits and behaviors to numb the pain of your fears, you're not only prolonging the pain but allowing it to gain strength and power over your life.

We spend so much time running away from our fears. We spend so much time trying not to look at them, to look anywhere else but directly in fear's face. As men, we will take on complex business assignments, intricate intellectual challenges, and strenuous physical tasks, to feel more in control, more in charge, more successful as men. Yet, we often flee from the kind of heavy digging and deep reflection required for internal undertakings of self-evaluation. We will go to the ends of the earth to uncover the truth about other things but will leave our own personal landscape as our one undiscovered country.

It is not possible to measure up to other people's expectations, because other people are not fair. Everyone comes with their own biases and misconceptions and shortsightedness and selfishness. This is true even of those people who truly do love you. People are not perfect, so the way they view you and your life and your future will not be perfect. When you allow another person to dictate the standards of your life, you have just abdicated enormous power to that individual, and you could spend the rest of your life hobbled by the burden of those expectations and crushed under the fear of failure.

Reaching Higher

Underlying this fear of inadequacy is the fear that, as a man, I am unlovable. Intimately aware of all my failings, a part of me is convinced that if people really knew the truth, they wouldn't love me. No amount of bravado, no amount of distraction, can totally remove that quiet-of-the-night fear. I desperately want to be worth something and am terrified I'm not.

Faith is where my fear of being unlovable meets God's assurance that he loves me. I call it an act of faith because it still wavers on the unbelievable that God, who knows me from the inside out with all my faults, still loves me. The way I am able to drive out my deepest fear of justifiable rejection is by setting my sights on God:

> Watch what God does, and then you do it, like children who learn proper behavior from their parents. Mostly what God does is love you. Keep company with him and learn a life of love. Observe how Christ loved us. His love was not cautious but extravagant. He didn't love in order to get something from us but to give everything of himself to us. Love like that.
>
> Ephesians 5:1–2 MSG

From a human perspective, love like this doesn't make sense. As an equation, love like this doesn't add up. From a rational point of view, love like this is illogical. After all, who hasn't been taught that if something seems too good to be true, it probably is? Love like this is not human; on our own, we can't do it. Love like this is not what man does; it is what God does. We're out of the human box altogether, which is why acknowledging and accepting this love is an act of faith.

11

Fear of Who You Are

It feels like I get up and put on a mask," he said wearily. I'd asked him what the hardest thing was about getting up every day. He'd come in for depression that was affecting his ability to function. He'd already tried his medical doctor but wasn't happy with the side effects of the antidepressant medication, which he said didn't help and made him feel worse. "Lately, the mask gets heavier and heavier. It's harder to put on every day."

"What kind of a mask?" I asked.

"I call it the Fine Mask," he said. "It's important to appear like everything's fine. The last thing I want is a bunch of questions or to have people think there's something wrong."

"So, you put on the Fine Mask for other people," I clarified.

"I've got a lot of people counting on me. It's important I project a certain image."

"But the mask is just that, isn't it, a projection?"

"People don't care if it's a projection," he objected, as if stating the obvious. "All they care about is that everything's fine. When

I'm at work, my supervisor doesn't want to hear there's a problem. He just wants to know everything's fine and my work will get done and I'll complete my job on time. When I'm at home, my kids sure don't want to know there's a problem. They just want to know everything's fine and they'll still have a roof over their heads, cell phones in their hands, and gas in their tanks." By the end of his speech, I could see the anger start to surface, but it was quickly replaced by what I assumed was the visual effect of the Fine Mask, a nondescript, flat look. The transition was quick.

"How long have you been wearing the Fine Mask?" I asked.

He chuckled once softly and produced the smallest of smiles. "A while."

Masquerade

Do you remember the story I told you back in the chapter on work, about the two men sizing each other up at the cocktail hour of a dinner party? That was an interesting party; most social parties are, at least the ones where you're with a bunch of people you're only marginally familiar with—the cocktail party type. In those social situations, people tend to show up wearing masks. Those masks can come down as the evening and the alcohol wear on, but unless you're completely comfortable with yourself as a person, the temptation to hide behind a mask of some sort is compelling. Believe me, I've felt the draw myself.

Usually, you can keep up appearances for a couple of hours if you watch what you say and how much you drink. You get in the car at the end of the night, take off your coat, loosen your tie, and breathe a sigh of relief. Finally, you can stop smiling and start farting. In other words, you get to be yourself, which means putting down the mask.

We all wear different masks for what I suspect is a single reason. In the last chapter, we talked about how compulsive behaviors can be used as a way to avoid living with fear—fear of failure, fear of not measuring up. Compulsive behaviors are an effective distraction from dealing with fear and its uncomfortable companions of anger, shame, and guilt, along with its uncomfortable consequences of anxiety, worry, and stress. Compulsive behaviors can also be used as masks, shielding others from learning the truth of that fear and shielding you from the necessity of acknowledging it.

Masks also allow you to project the preferred image of yourself. Behind the mask, you feel safe. The mask hides the fear you want to keep hidden and projects a false image in its place. The difficulty is, though, the more the fear grows, the bigger the mask needed to cover it and the stronger the need for the compulsive behavior to mask the fear. It's a vicious cycle.

Unmasked

No matter how much time you spend viewing pornography, it is not improving your sex life. No matter how much time and energy you devote to feeding your anger, it doesn't dissipate. No matter how much time you spend invested in online gaming and fantasy events, they will never produce real-life dividends, with real situations and real people. No matter how much time you spend at work, work is never done. No matter how much time you spend sheltering yourself from others, you can't make yourself safe. No matter how many lies you tell to yourself and others, you can't run from the truth. No matter how much you try to fill yourself up from the outside, you can never fill the hole on the inside. No matter how many times you compete with other people, you can't make yourself a winner. Behind all of that behavior, behind all of those masks, is a truth you need to come to grips with. After years of working in this field, I can assure you it's better for you to unmask yourself than to wait for someone else to do it for you.

A couple of years ago, a very successful man was publically unmasked. He had been in business for fifty years, garnering phenomenal commercial success, personal wealth, and power. His mask projected an image of a man able to produce amazing investment returns, even in difficult markets. Many people, both individuals and charitable organizations, believed the mask and turned over their life savings to the man to invest. He was well known in New York and London, all around the world. He was a player, a power broker—that was his mask. Underneath, it turned out, was a crook.

This man did not unmask himself. Instead, his sons went to the authorities. At the time, there was speculation that the reason the sons came forward was to preempt being charged themselves, as this man's financial house of cards was beginning to tumble. Regardless of the motives, as the truth began to see the light, the size of this man's mask was revealed, and the nation gave a collective gasp. The man's name is Bernard Madoff. His true identify is a thief, the creator of the largest investment Ponzi scheme in United States history, estimated at defrauding investors of billions of dollars.

For years, Madoff was extremely successful at his masquerade as an investment broker. The court-appointed trustee of the people and institutions Madoff defrauded, Irving Picard, in an interview with *60 Minutes*'s Morley Safer, said he wasn't even sure Madoff had ever been a legitimate trader. If Picard is right, that's 50 years of living behind a mask. Madoff was convicted of fraud and is sitting in a North Carolina jail for 150 years or until his death, whichever comes first. The negative shock waves of Madoff's unmasking continued past his incarceration. Last year, Madoff's oldest son, Mark, committed suicide in his New York apartment, with his two-year-old son sleeping nearby.[7]

Masks start out as a way to protect you and end up causing a great deal of damage. Granted, there are very few men in the world with as large and deceptive a mask as Bernard Madoff. He'll go down in history, unfortunately, for the size of his mask. All of us, though, flirt with masks. We have our public face and our private face. We have our work face and our family face. We often tailor our responses and attitudes and behaviors to match those we're with, often treating the people we know the least with the most civility.

Phil McGraw, the former psychologist turned television host, is credited as saying, "We all have a social mask, right? We put it on, we go out, put our best foot forward, our best image. But behind that social mask is a personal truth, what we really, really believe about who we are and what we're capable of."[8] Some people never drop the mask because of a fear of who they really are and a denial of what they're really capable of.

Why should we as men be so fearful of who we are? I believe this powerful fear comes from a terror of showing weakness. Men often wear masks to hide personal weakness. Men will wear a mask of competency, of normalcy, of nonchalance, of Fine, while terrified that others might learn they are really none of the above.

I have such admiration for Twelve-Step programs and Alcoholics Anonymous in particular. One of the first acts a participant involved in an AA meeting does is take off the mask and declare the truth of who he is. "Hi, my name is _____ and I'm an alcoholic." It is both a terrifying and a freeing experience to admit to yourself and others an essential truth about yourself. It is an empowering experience to accept and be accepted for who you really are—no masks.

Some men are fearful of showing who they really are because of the false pride of perfectionism. They have been sold a bill of goods about what manhood means and constantly compare themselves to those standards. Usually, they have grown up in a household with very rigid rules and an emotionally withdrawn or distant father. This is not a household with a father as buddy, as mentor. It is a household with father as judge.

Some men are fearful of showing who they are because they have never learned to accept who they are. These men have never undergone the father-son rite of passage, the manhood transfer, in an organic, natural way. Perhaps their fathers were not available to them physically or emotionally. Perhaps the manhood template being handed down from father to son was flawed, a generational corruption in the file of manhood. Sometimes, an explanation of the essential elements of manhood, of character and sacrifice, of respect for self and others, is not a conversation that ever occurs between father and son. There is power in verbal acknowledgment and reinforcement, through conversation between father and son. How strange that a father will feel compelled to explain physical sex to his son but neglect to provide the entire male context. It's as if the father considers his son's manhood to be relegated to a single body organ instead of encompassing his son's identity. It is such shortsightedness that leaves sons to grow up as adult men, blinded by an inability to understand and fearful of who they really are.

Taking Charge

As I said before, we all wear masks. Sometimes, it's for as inconsequential a reason as being able to get through a dinner party. Sometimes, it's to find a way—any way—to not be who we really are so we can get through the day. All of us, I think, fall somewhere between those two spectrums. I also said that it's best if you unmask yourself, so that's what I'd like you to do now.

For those of you who are artistically gifted or don't really care that you're not, I'd like you to think about the various masks you wear. If you have trouble identifying them, think about yourself, who you are, and how you act in various social situations. Then, draw your masks on a piece of paper. The man I told you about at the start of this chapter had a Fine Mask, a bland, nothing's-wrong-but-don't-ask-me-about-it face he put on in the morning to keep people and his fears at bay.

For those of you who just throw in the towel on anything artistic, you're not off the hook because you can't or won't draw. Instead, I'd like you to find examples of what your masks look like by finding similar expressions on other people. The easiest way to do this used to be pictures in magazines, but many people don't subscribe to paper anymore. Now, you can google images of people looking happy or smug or bored or angry or whatever expression you want. Find one that matches your Fine Mask or whatever you call your mask or masks and print it out.

You should now look at each mask and answer the following questions:

- How long have you been wearing this mask?
- How often do you put it on?
- Do you wear it out in public, or is it reserved for a certain individual?
- Do you remember anyone else wearing a similar mask?
- Did you grow up in a household where family members often wore masks?
- How do you feel when you wear the mask?
- What specifically are you trying to obscure by wearing the mask?

- Do you have a name for this mask, like the Fine Mask?
- Do you make sure to wear this mask during certain activities? Where and why?
- Do you make sure to wear this mask around certain people? Who and why?
- What activities or behaviors that you engage in help strengthen the mask?
- Have you ever been unmasked? If so, by whom, and what happened?

In AA, you have to unmask yourself and speak the truth. That requires a great deal of courage, but before that it usually requires a great deal of pain. Masks keep pain hidden. Hidden pain remains. The way to be free of your pain is to stop hiding from it. Freedom from pain comes by facing it, naming it, and finding a way through it.

As men we have always challenged ourselves by enduring painful tasks. I think of those training for a marathon or a triathlon. It takes courage and fortitude to face the physical pain and challenge, to persevere and triumph. I admire men who accomplish these difficult physical tasks.

I also greatly admire men who challenge themselves to endure the painful task of removing their masks. When these masks are lifted, there are usually no crowds cheering, no accolades or medals. Sometimes, the only other person to witness the struggle, the persistence and the victory, is me. I have never been to an Olympic event, but I've witnessed some herculean contests of pain, of will, of courage, of fortitude in the quiet corner of my office. I don't give out medals. In fact, victory usually means the eventual end to our professional relationship, and I wouldn't have it any other way.

Reaching Higher

Masks are really elaborate lies meant to protect us from the truth. At first, the mask seems to be a good thing, keeping us safe. It's meant to be worn, just a little while, in this particular situation, as a precaution. Masks, however, have a way of becoming more permanent. They are easy to put on and difficult to take off. Instead of keeping to the role of protector, masks can get used to the spotlight and demand center stage more and more of the time until you're not sure what the truth is anymore.

Lies used to cover the truth are dangerous. The more consequential the truth, the bigger the mask becomes and the more dangerous the lie. Even with huge masks, the truth has a way of peeking out; just ask Bernie Madoff. Or you could ask Jesus:

> You can't keep your true self hidden forever; before long you'll be exposed. You can't hide behind a religious mask forever; sooner or later the mask will slip and your true face will be known.
>
> Luke 12:2 MSG

Here, Jesus was talking about a phony mask of self-righteousness, but you can substitute any kind of mask you want. Sooner or later, the mask will slip and your true face will be known. Sometimes, the last person to realize the mask has slipped is you; others have been aware of your true self peeking out while you've been furiously trying to hold up a slipping mask.

God wants you to put down your masks, not because he wants you to be hurt or humiliated but because he wants you to walk in the truth. John 8:32 says that the truth will set you free. Masks are a form of bondage because they require effort and energy to maintain. God wants you to stop hiding from yourself and from him.

PART 3

THE HOW

12

Accept What Is

"You can't go back and change thirty-plus years of history," I told him.

"I know," Colin replied. "I just wish things could have been different."

"Have you heard the old saying about wishes?" I asked him.

"You mean the one that goes 'If wishes were horses, beggars would ride'?" Obviously, he was familiar.

"Yeah, that's the one," I said, without giving any further explanation.

Colin was silent for a minute and then said, "So, what are you saying? I'm a beggar?"

I nodded. "In a way."

"How am I a beggar?" I could tell he was offended by the comparison.

"Beggars wait for other people to solve their problems." I let that sink in a bit before I continued. "Colin, your dad is not going to change. What I'm saying is you have to base your life on more

185

than wishing he would. If you wait for other people to act before you can move forward, you won't."

He thought some more and then admitted, "Okay, I'm stuck. I want so badly to go back and rewrite my life, but I can't. I keep waiting for something, some sort of opening, to force what I know to be true to be wrong. Because it is wrong!" He ran out of steam. "At least, it's not right."

"You're right. What happened to you was wrong. You never should have been treated that way. In a perfect world, what happened to you wouldn't have. But this isn't a perfect world, and it did happen to you. Your challenge is not to try to re-create the past; that's not possible. Your challenge is to accept the past and use it to make a better future for yourself and your family."

It was my turn to wait. I wanted to see if he would revert back to blame and excuses and staying in the past. That was familiar territory. He knew that place backwards and forwards. The future, detached from that past, was the unknown. I waited to see which he would choose—past or future.

He sat, eyes down, deciding. *Come on*, I thought to myself while I waited. *Do it.*

"My problem isn't my dad," he finally said.

"Well, actually, he's a big part of it," I countered. "Your dad is your problem, but he's not your solution; you are. You need to stop waiting for him to apologize or to even know he needs to. That's a beggar's wish. You need to go out and get your own horse."

Accept Who You Are

It's difficult to accept who we are, how life has shaped us, and what we've done in response. We wish we could be better than we are, but if we're honest, we know we're not. So we give up on being honest. We spend a great deal of time pretending we're someone we're not, looking anywhere other than at the man in the mirror. When we look in the mirror and see imperfection and weakness and failure, we cringe. We prefer our diversions, our compulsions, our masks, to the awful truth that we're less than we should be.

There are a lot of reasons why we're less than we should be. Some of those reasons are on us. Some of them are on others. There are things in our past that mess us up. There are relationships that drive us crazy. There are mistakes and habits we just can't seem to get over. Somewhere along the line we were taught that putting on the Fine Mask and hiding out in a man cave was the way to get beyond that knot in the pit of our stomachs when we fail to measure up and know it.

So we work and we play, we act and we move, trying to outrun the gut check. Some of us are pretty successful at running; it takes years for bone-deep fear to catch up to us. In the interim, we often damage our relationships and screw up our health. We spend so much time running from truth, we're not really sure what it is anymore.

Acceptance is the point at which you stop running. Acceptance is taking that long, hard look in the mirror and ruthlessly cataloging who you are. There's a funny thing about acceptance, though. Only you can do it for yourself. It doesn't really count if other people accept you—that's nice, of course—but acceptance only really works when you accept yourself.

The goal of acceptance is not to stand still, to stay stuck in your compulsions, happy behind your masks. The goal of acceptance is to designate your true starting point so you can begin to move away from being stuck and toward positive change. For instance, if you are an alcoholic, acceptance is that starting point when you say, "Hi, my name is _____ and I'm an alcoholic." Once you accept you're an alcoholic, you accept what is. That truth, that starting point, alters where you go from there. If you are an alcoholic, you cannot drink alcohol, period. You cannot put yourself into a position of temptation where alcohol is concerned. Does accepting you're an alcoholic mean you admit weakness? Absolutely, but admitting you're weak is not so you can beat yourself up. Admitting the truth defines your starting point on a journey to sobriety that leads to understanding who you are, making amends for past mistakes, learning how to live a new life free of addiction, and helping other people do the same.

So, you tell me which life is more characterized by weakness: the alcoholic hiding behind a mask, refusing to admit the truth and continuing to degrade his life through drinking—or the alcoholic who admits his weakness and uses that admission to craft a new, sober life. I know who's got my vote.

Maybe your particular battle isn't booze—but by now you know what that battle is. Just substitute what you're battling for alcohol. Weakness happens; failure happens; life happens. You are not immune, no matter what you were led to believe growing up or what you've been telling yourself ever since. It's time to accept the starting point of your battle and begin to figure out what you're going to do, besides pretending the battle doesn't exist or using it as an excuse to stay hidden behind your masks. Admitting weakness means accepting not only the starting point of your weakness but what you've done in your life to protect that weakness. As a man, as someone who's supposed to be protecting others, it can be a challenge to admit that shielding your weakness has meant exposing others to harm.

Baggage

It's one thing to admit you've messed up and to accept your true starting place because of what you've done. It can be another thing altogether to accept your true starting place because of what someone else has done to you. This was Colin's dilemma. Colin did not want to accept the truth of who he was because it meant having to admit the truth of who his father was.

This sort of hesitancy is not displayed by men alone. Both men and women have difficulty accepting the truth of who they are because it requires recognition of the truth of what has happened to them. Acknowledging they were ever in such a state of vulnerability in the past leaves them feeling extremely vulnerable in the present. Acknowledging the truth that lightning has struck once in their lives leaves them fearful of lightning striking twice. In this world full of unfairness and injustice, lightning strikes all the time.

When a child has been abused, neglected, or abandoned, that child will often internalize the reasons and make himself responsible for it. In order to provide stability to a chaotic world, a child will internalize the chaos. He will attempt to control the uncontrollable by making himself responsible. Then he has a sense of security that if he is smart enough or good enough or obedient enough, the pain will stop. But stopping the pain is only the first part of that security equation. The second part is if he is smart enough or good enough or obedient enough, not only will the bad end but the good will start. Every abused child desperately longs for a two-part world, a world without pain and a world with love. Even if he can have the first world, a world devoid of pain, he still longs for a world with love.

I remember another situation, in which I was trying to help a man understand and accept his true starting point. This man had no problem admitting that his past was difficult; there was really no way around it, given what he had suffered as a child. He told me the pain was gone—he was over it, and the pain had made him stronger for surviving it. He treated the pain like a banner instead

189

of a burden. This man was willing to live in a one-part world, the world of no more pain. However, the unhealed wound remained fresh and raw whenever he ventured close to that second-part world, the world where love is supposed to exist. The pain was over, but the love never happened. So, in the second world, a void continued to exist. This man did not want to go anywhere near that second world of love because, when he did, he felt weak. In his mind, love became entangled with weakness. He had great difficulty expressing his feelings, experiencing intimacy, and demonstrating love and forgiveness to others. In his mind, that second-part world of love was carefully locked away, and it was difficult to get him to budge.

I was running out of visuals to illustrate my point, to allow him to connect with the pain he kept so carefully locked away. After trying several examples that didn't work, I decided on luggage. (This was back when the term "baggage" was first used as a metaphor for the difficult past people carry with them in the present.) Thinking about baggage, I asked him if he could go anywhere on a vacation with his family, where would he go. He said he'd like to go to Hawaii sometime because of the sun.

"Okay, you're going to Hawaii," I began. "How many bags do you think you'll need to take?"

I could tell he was confused by the question. "I don't know, um, at least one."

"Oh, you think you've only got one bag? You've got a lot more than that," I told him. "Every time you go anywhere you bring along the baggage of your past. You're carting around so much old stuff, you barely have the strength to carry even one present bag."

"I'm strong enough to handle both," he assured me, clearly angry at my insinuation of his inability.

"Okay, let's say you are strong enough to carry around all your past along with your present. How much time and energy and resources does that take? How much of your life is left over for anything or anyone else? Should I ask your wife? Should I ask your kids?"

"What I went through made me who I am today," he stated. "I'm not ashamed of it, and I'm not going to run from it."

"I'm not asking you to run from it. I'm asking you to put it down so you can take other things up."

"If I'm just supposed to put it down, just forget about it, then what was all that for?" He wasn't happy with where I was going.

"You've been carrying a heavy load for a lot of years." I tried a different analogy. "Say you were a weight lifter. After years and years of lifting weights, what would be the outcome?"

"Muscles," he spat out, irritated. Now I was relegated to single word answers and a don't-mess-with-me stare. Fair enough.

"Does a weight lifter still have those muscles when he puts down the weights?" I had him, and he knew it.

"Yes," he conceded slowly. "But if he doesn't keep lifting, he'll lose his muscles." Now he thought he had me.

"But he doesn't have to keep lifting the same set of weights, does he? Once he's developed the muscles, he can use them to lift other things." Checkmate.

I leaned in and lowered my voice. "I'm not asking you to give up the strength you've gained from what you've suffered. I'm asking you to use the strength you've gained to start lifting other things besides your suffering."

"What other things am I supposed to start lifting?"

Finally.

I knew he was thinking of present things, like his relationship with his wife and kids, but there was something from his past that still needed to be dealt with. "How about lifting your grief? You've spent so much time angry, headlocking your pain, that you haven't allowed yourself to grieve what was done to you. I know you've survived it, but you haven't grieved it."

"What's the point of grieving it now?" he asked, still angry. "Crying about it can't change it."

"You're right," I agreed. "Grieving can't change it, but grieving can change *you*."

The *E* and *F* Words

I'm not sure you've picked up on it, but I've tried hard to refrain from too much use of the *E* and *F* words—*emotions* and *feelings*. Men are often suspicious (I would never say fearful) of feelings and emotions. Emotions and feelings are for women, the result of PMS and other female issues. Feelings make you weak. Emotions make you lose control. Emotions and feelings open up windows into personal areas you don't want viewed by others. Men can yell and scream and rant, but we should never, ever shed tears. We can sweat and strain, but tears are kept in reserve for those few situations in which they're deemed appropriate, like death—but only the death of beloved pets or close family members. Otherwise, tears are suspect, just as emotions and feelings are suspect. Emotions are, well, an emotional, spontaneous response, not a logical, measured, reasoned response. Feelings are a, well, feeling and not an action.

Acceptance of who you are as a man includes accepting that you are an emotional person with feelings. Granted, your emotional responses will not mimic those of women, but that doesn't mean you don't have them. When did we get the idea men aren't supposed to cry? I suppose it happened back in childhood, when it became apparent that girls cried a lot more than boys. Since we didn't want to be called a girl, we learned to supress any emotional response that wasn't part of boy culture. We learned it was fine to be angry, frustrated, worried—but watch out for profound sadness or becoming emotionally overwhelmed. Choose anything else, do anything else, to avoid tears. It's okay to blink away a few tears if you're really, really hurt, but don't even think about a full-blown sob. Suck it up, walk it off, shake it out, turn your head, blink your eyes, cuss. Stuff the pain firmly in the past if you can, and if you can't, deal with the pain in private.

Emotions and feelings don't stuff very well. They're pretty good at festering, and they don't really go away. Stuffed emotions have a tendency to break out in things like compulsive behaviors. That is why it's vital for you to understand who you are on an emotional level and how you express yourself emotionally, both overtly and covertly. It's important for you to understand your emotional triggers and why punching those particular buttons produces the response it does. Unacknowledged emotions can swing out of control. Understanding your emotions, where they come from, the feelings they provoke, and why you react the way you do, is part of accepting who you are.

Men generally don't like to talk about emotions or feelings for a couple of reasons, I've found. The first reason is because emotions are confusing. Women seem able to immediately identify emotions, what they're feeling and why. Women exhibit a sort of emotional clarity. Many men, however, find emotions to be murky. It's harder to find the center of them, and it takes longer to ferret them out. Many men would rather not bother for what I've found is the second reason: they generally don't like to talk about emotions because that talk can get emotional. When you finally lance the festering sore, it hurts.

Digging into your emotions provokes an emotional response, and sometimes that response is strong. If a man becomes angry with me in session, that man will apologize about a third of the time. But if a man becomes tearful in session, he will immediately apologize almost every time. Tears are a male social faux pas, even in a setting where tears would normally, at least from a female point of view, seem completely appropriate. Men have joked with me about coming into contact with their feminine side after shedding a tear or two (after the mortification has passed and somehow the world didn't end).

In order to *accept* who you are, you need to *know* who you are, including who you are emotionally. There is no shame in accepting yourself as an emotional person. Emotions are not something to hide from or to stuff away in the back recesses of your thoughts. Emotions don't go away, nor should they.

So, to recap, acceptance is a vigorous endeavor, if you haven't figured that out already. To accept yourself, you need to:

- accept what's happened to you in the past
- accept how that past has shaped you
- accept what you've done in response to that past
- accept your emotional response to all of the above

Until you've accepted these aspects of your past, you won't be ready to deal with your present or direct your future. You'll continue to be led around by your past. That's a lousy position to be in.

Once you've put your past into perspective, you've attained the necessary vantage point to survey your present. Once you know where you actually are, it's a lot easier to figure out where you need to go and how you need to get there.

The Power to Change

- *Change requires clarity*. If you can't see what's broken, you don't know what to fix. If you don't know what to fix, you can't decide how to fix it.

- *Change requires action.* Once you've recognized something's broken and decide what you need to do to fix it, you must act.

- *Change requires strategic action.* This is where some men go offtrack. They recognize the need to change and experience the imperative to act but fail to act strategically. Instead of acting in a way that produces positive change, they act simply as a way to keep moving, often in a way that perpetuates the problem instead of eliminating it.

- *Change requires submission.* Submission is not a manly word. Submission means capitulation, surrender, compliance. It is the opposite of being your own man, charting your own course, being the captain of your own ship. Yet, even a ship's captain must submit to a new course in order to change direction. Has he stopped being the captain because he's changed course? Of course not. He has surveyed his bearings, the current conditions, the potential for those conditions to change; he has evaluated the consequences to his ship, his cargo, and his crew of staying the course or changing direction. A ship's captain is in charge of the decision to change even when he is not in charge of the conditions requiring change. A wise captain accepts the reality of his position and submits to the prevailing conditions by adjusting course. Unwise captains plow ahead and end up wrecking ships.

Taking Charge

Acceptance should be a change agent in your life. The truth that naturally flows from knowing who you are can be a mighty wind. You can fight against it and wreck your ship, or you can accept it and find a way to use that energy to chart a new course.

Charting a new course for your life isn't only about where you want to go; it's also about who you want to be when you get there. Where do you want to go and who do you want to be? Using the ship analogy, please visualize the following:

- Your ship is your life. All ships have a name; what's yours?
- All ships have a point of christening, a launch date when they first take to the water. This christening point is when you finally felt in charge of your life. Where was that? When was that?
- When your ship first left dock, where was it headed?
- Your course is the result of the decisions you've made in your life. Are you still headed in your original direction? If so, what has helped you stay the course? If not, what has caused you to go in a different direction?
- Your cargo is the material goods you've accumulated in your travels through life. How attached are you to this cargo? Are you willing to jettison all or part in order to change course?
- Your ballast is the baggage you've accumulated over the years. Are you willing to examine this ballast and rearrange it if necessary to maximize your potential to reach port?
- Your crew are those people who are sailing with you, both family and friends. Who on this crew is your first mate? What has your first mate been telling you about the course you're on?
- Reality is the prevailing conditions. When you think about these conditions, remember to include not only external conditions like weather (what's going on around you that you can't control), water depth (how much cushion you have between you and adverse consequences), and wave action (how much resistance you are experiencing on your current course) but also internal conditions like the morale of your crew (relationships

196

with family and friends) and the seaworthiness of your ship (what on board your life is creating a danger).

When you're out on the water, you place yourself in an inherently dangerous situation. On the water, who you are matters because who you are affects what you do. It's no different in life. In an inherently dangerous situation, decisions have consequences. What you do matters.

Can you imagine the sheer folly of a ship's captain, in the midst of a storm, huddling in his cabin playing chess? Yet men do the same thing all the time. They live their lives amid a storm—career in a shambles, relationships falling apart, health shaky—and they sit inside their cabins playing video games, viewing pornography, work emailing, drinking or eating themselves into oblivion while outside the winds rage. Instead of tackling the challenges life presents, they prefer the easy win of the known and comfortable. This is a surefire way to end up splintered on the rocks.

If this has been you in the past, it's time to come out of your cabin. It's time to walk the deck of your ship, fully engaged and ready to take command. It's time to inspect the soundness of your vessel, the morale of your crew, the security of your cargo, the positioning of your ballast. It's time to survey the prevailing conditions and think ahead to what might be coming over the next horizon. A ship is meant to be captained and a life is meant to be lived. Neither is easy—but what an adventure!

Reaching Higher

Earlier I talked about my admiration for Twelve-Step programs. Part of this admiration comes from their fearless acceptance of what *is*, right from the get-go. No hemming and hawing. No spin or attempting to temper the truth. The first step just lays out the truth for all to see: "My name is Gregg and I'm powerless." In this human condition, powerless is what is.

In the paradox of confession, such an admission of weakness leads to strength. Granted, the first step is to admit "I am powerless," but the journey doesn't stop there. Eleven steps remain. During those eleven steps, "I am powerless" is transformed into "I am powerless, but God and I together are not powerless; God and I together are powerful enough to overcome this addiction."

I want you to be honest here. Are you the type of person who needs to do everything yourself? If you're doing a project and someone comes in to provide needed help, does that negate the accomplishment of completing the project? Are victories tainted if they're not solo? If you're such an individual, accepting what is will be difficult because the truth is, there will be times when you are powerless and you will need strength from outside yourself to accomplish a challenging task. If it has to be only you, you will fail. When you accept this reality, you open the door to collaborative victory and success.

There is someone who wants to be a part of your victories and successes in life. He altered course himself, taking on human form and living as a man. His name is Jesus and he is God, yes, but he is also a man, just like you. Jesus had to accept some difficult realities—going from heaven to a cattle trough, hunger and pain and doubt and want, rejection from those he came to save, gaining his victory only through death. As a man, Jesus could not have done this alone; he realized his success through his relationship with God, paving the way to show you how it can be done. The writer of Hebrews says this about him:

> Now that we know what we have—Jesus, this great high priest with access to God—let's not let it slip through our fingers. We

don't have a priest who is out of touch with our reality. He's been through weakness and testing, experienced it all—all but the sin. So let's walk right up to him and get what he's so ready to give. Take the mercy, accept the help.

Hebrews 4:14 MSG

Accept what is. Accept God's help and mercy. Are you powerless? Yes, but you and God together are strong enough to claim victory.

13

Love Yourself Enough to Say No

Who loves you?" I asked Wes. We were looking over the pictures he'd posted on his Facebook page. There looked to be hundreds of pictures, shots of Wes engaged in rock climbing, kayaking, camping, or hiking, but relatively few of Wes with people.

I could tell Wes found my question to be completely out of left field. Earlier, I'd asked him to tell me about himself, which he'd summed up in about three sentences. It wasn't nearly enough, but I figured getting information out of him would be like extracting gold from a played-out mine—a modest outcome for a great deal of effort.

When I asked if he was on Facebook, his eyes lit up. He said he was, so we went to my computer and he logged in. At first, he sort of apologized for the content of some of his wall posts, but I just shrugged those off. I was interested in his pictures. He had so many. I mentally tried to calculate the amount of time and effort it would take to put together such an impressive collection. Wes was clearly proud of the portrait these pictures presented of him as strong, athletic, and capable. He appeared to enjoy an intense relationship with the outdoors, but I didn't detect the same sort of intensity where people were concerned.

So, I asked, "Who loves you?" Wes was taken aback, and I could see a defensive wall rise up as his demeanor went flat.

"You mean right now?" he clarified, as a way to put off answering while he tried to figure out what I was after.

"Sure, who loves you right now?" I agreed, intrigued by his desire to place this question into a time frame.

"Well, my daughters do. You saw them. They're eight and eleven. Even though I'm divorced, I'm still a part of my kids' lives." I remembered seeing some pictures of the girls on Facebook, but Wes wasn't in very many of them.

"That's good." I nodded in encouragement because he'd leaned back in his chair, away from me. The camaraderie we'd shared over Facebook was over. "Who else?"

"Hmm . . . my mom," he said as if stating the obvious. Then, to preempt my next question, he continued, "My dad died last year." Of course, he didn't exactly say whether or not his father had loved him, but I decided not to go down that particular path at that moment.

"Do you have any other family?"

"I've got a sister and a brother. My sister's older and my brother's younger. I guess they love me." He shrugged his shoulders. "We don't really talk about that much. My sister's got her own family, and my brother and I don't really keep in touch, except on Facebook. That just isn't something we talk about."

"Okay, so far you've mentioned members of your immediate family." He still didn't know where I was going but must have considered the line of questioning innocuous enough to continue. "Anyone else love you?"

"Um . . . not at the moment. I'm not in a relationship with any-one." Finally, he said what he'd been thinking the whole time. "Why do you ask?"

"I wanted to see if you'd say yourself."

Wes was puzzled and not a little bit frustrated. "You want to know if I love *myself*?" I could have been speaking Latin and it would have made more sense.

"Yes. Of all the people who love you, the most important one is you." Wes shrugged again, shook his head, and narrowed his eyes in confusion.

Wes, like other men I've worked with, considered self-love to be one of those touchy-feely female concepts. What did it matter for a guy if he loved himself? Wes told me loving himself was the furthest thing from his mind when he got up in the morning. He just went out and did his job and lived his life. He didn't need to go around complimenting himself and patting himself on the back.

Self-promotion was his definition of self-love, which was evi-denced by his Facebook page. His gallery of photos seemed promo-tional, self-congratulatory. Looking through them, I saw a guy who needed to show definitive proof of his value and worth through the things he accomplished. Wes didn't realize it, but those pictures were self-promotion, not self-love. They were a way to compliment him-self, pat himself on the back, and tell himself what a great person—at least, what a great athlete—he was. The very things Wes said he didn't need were the very things he made sure he did for himself.

Wes confused self-promotion with self-love and denied both. But people who feel loved by others generally don't have to devote so much energy to promoting themselves. People who truly love themselves generally don't need to create extensive exhibits of their value and worth. We men have a way of promoting ourselves, but we don't always find a way to love ourselves.

The Logic of Love

As men, we take pride in our ability to reach conclusions and take action based on logic and rationality. In the midst of this concrete decision making, something considered to be subjective, such as self-love, can appear out of place. I contend, however, that it is both logical and rational to love yourself.

Wes confused self-love with self-promotion because that's what he experienced growing up. As a child, love was equated with performance. Love was not something given; love was something earned. According to Wes, his father loved him when Wes was able to demonstrate he did well, that he performed up to expectations. If Wes did not perform well, love was withheld. Wes claimed he understood that model and agreed with it.

"Why should I receive love if I don't earn it?" he asked during one of our sessions. "What good is love if it doesn't motivate you to do your best?"

"I suppose that would work," I told him, "if people could always do their best. But they can't."

"People can always choose to do their best," Wes retorted in a tone that indicated no argument was possible. "Why should they be rewarded when they don't?"

"Love isn't a reward, like throwing a dog a treat when it does something clever. Love is a decision to bond to that dog even when it acts like a dog." I remembered seeing some pictures of a younger Wes with a golden retriever. "What was the name of your dog growing up?"

"Digger." He smiled. "I think we named him Apollo at first, but Digger's the name that stuck."

"Was that the dog I saw in those pictures of you as a teenager?"
"Yeah."
"His name was . . . *Digger*," I confirmed.

"Yeah." His face went serious. I could only envision the breadth and depth of the destruction this dog must have accomplished in the family to have arrived at such a descriptive name. By the look on Wes's face, he was remembering Digger too, but I doubted he was thinking about how bad a dog he was.

"His name was Digger, and you loved him anyway. Aren't you at least as worthy of love as your dog?"

It was easier for Wes to talk about his dog than himself. Wes loved that dog, even though it dug everywhere in the yard, uprooting plants and making a giant mess. Even when Digger ate his socks, Wes still loved him.

"Wait, didn't Digger know he wasn't supposed to eat your socks? You said he was a smart dog."

"Oh, he was smart. He knew he wasn't supposed to, but he was just a dog."

"And you're just a person, Wes. Sometimes you know you shouldn't do something, and you do it anyway. When it was Digger, you forgave him and still loved him. Why can't you do that for yourself?"

One Good Reason

When engaged in battle, it's imperative that you consider yourself worthy of survival. You should go into battle meaning to come out of it at the end, trying your very best to be victorious even if it's only you at stake. I have been disheartened by how many men give up on their battles in life because, deep down, they don't think they're worth the effort to win. When you give up on yourself, you ensure defeat.

Change is a battle. It takes effort and fortitude. Many of the behaviors discussed in this book produce some sort of value, even a perverse one. These behaviors provide comfort or distraction or sexual gratification or personal accomplishment. These are the reasons why you've adopted the behaviors in the first place. These are the reasons why you continue to do them even when you know you should change.

The only way to free yourself from the behavior and those steel-cabled reasons is to find something strong enough to sever the connection. All you need to find is one good reason. I have watched people fight addictive behaviors for spouses, for parents, for children. While those are powerful reasons, they often aren't strong enough to overcome the force of the addiction. Ultimately, you cannot change for anyone else. You've got to decide to change for yourself, because you are worth the effort. You realize you're worth the effort only when you decide to love yourself—not your performance or your abilities or your accomplishments—but to love yourself *for* yourself.

Saying No

Loving yourself is not presenting yourself with carte blanche to do whatever you want. On the contrary, true self-love allows you to deny yourself. The ultimate self-love is tough love, because there are few things tougher in life than telling yourself no when what you want to say is yes. In order to act in a mature way, you need to be able to truly evaluate the cost-benefit scenario on any activity, behavior, or pattern in your life. On one side of the equation is the value of what you want to do. On the other side is your value. If you misinterpret the value on either side, you won't come up with the correct answer. When you devalue yourself as a person, then the cost-benefit ratio is skewed and those detrimental patterns, activities, and behaviors are credited with more value than they're worth because you're credited with less. The only way to fight the pull of those behaviors is to have a strong grasp on what's really—and who's really—at stake.

When I was in high school, I couldn't wait to hit eighteen. Eighteen meant graduation and freedom, freedom from all the things my parents kept telling me no to. Adulthood meant saying yes. It didn't take me long my freshman year of college to figure out it was much easier to say yes than it was to say no. I said yes and stayed up too late. I said yes and put off doing my homework until the last minute. I said yes and hung out with friends instead of getting my shopping or my laundry done. I said yes and ended up tired, stressed out about my classes, and constantly behind on mundane stuff. There was no one to blame but myself.

That's when I learned that being an adult is less about saying yes than it is about saying no. College is where I really learned that responsibility comes with a price. I had to decide if I, through my education, was worth saying no. Because I wanted to do well in school, I said no to some very fun things. Don't get me wrong, I still said yes to many, but I couldn't say yes to all of them and still achieve what I wanted for myself.

That lesson has never really stopped playing itself out in my life. If I want to spend time with my wife, I need to say no to working late all the time. If I want to spend time with my kids, I need to say no to staying constantly connected to all my tech gadgets. If I want to spend time with my God, I have to say no to sleeping in or skipping church. I have to choose what's best for me and not always what I want to do or what feels good at the time. If I just did what feels good, I'd probably be four hundred pounds, because I really enjoy eating.

I do all these things that aren't always what I want to do, because I love myself. Yes, I love my wife and my kids and my God, but the starting point for my love for others is my ability to love myself. If I can't really love the person I'm the closest to—myself—how am I supposed to know how to truly love anyone else?

When you withhold the gift of love from yourself, it's easier to look to other things to fill the void.

If you don't really love yourself, you'll work yourself to death trying to earn that love.

If you don't really love yourself, you'll give in to pale substitutes, like pornography and promiscuity, for true intimacy.

If you don't really love yourself, you'll continue scraping your horns against other people in sarcastic, competitive jousting and deny yourself real friendship.

If you don't really love yourself, there won't be enough food or drink to compensate.

If you don't really love yourself, you'll never stop being angry at yourself and venting that anger on others.

If you don't really love yourself, you'll never be comfortable showing love to others.

If you don't really love yourself, you'll constantly find ways to hide from the truth.

Taking Charge

It's time for you to come up with your own One Good Reason to change your life. I understand it's much easier to look to loved ones or outside circumstances for reasons to change. All of those are beneficial, but you've got to come up with a reason that starts with you and loving yourself. For each behavior, activity, or attitude you know you need to change, I want you to make a Reasons

List. The first one, the One Good Reason, at the top of the list needs to be about you. Go ahead and list all of those other reasons underneath—but until you decide you're worth it, it's going to be difficult to find the motivation for sustained, long-term change.

My Reasons List
One Good Reason:

Other Reason:

Other Reason:

Other Reason:

Other Reason:

Other Reason:

There's a reason why expending this effort and energy to change is worth it—and that's because you are worth it. You may not have been taught or told or modeled that you were worth it, but the time has come for you to approach yourself as a loving, mature adult. Other adults may have withheld love from you or made a mess of how they loved you, but you can decide to love yourself. You don't have to prove that love or promote that love, but you do have to accept that love. Loving yourself isn't a weakness; loving yourself is a wellspring of strength. Loving yourself becomes the springboard you use to dive into a true love for others.

Reaching Higher

Still not convinced you're worth loving? God, through Christ, went out of his way to provide definitive proof. John 3:16 says: "For God so loved the world that he gave his one and only Son, that whoever believes in him shall not perish but have eternal life." There's the proof, right there—the death of Christ. Now, many men understand the death part. They have condemned themselves to a slow, drawn-out death by the activities they engage in. They may not be killing off their bodies, but they're killing off their joy, their hope, their sense of worth, their relationships. But death isn't the point of this verse; life is. God's goal wasn't to kill his Son to prove to you how much you deserve death. God's goal was to create an attitude of belief that leads to victory over death. Christ died for my sins, yes, but he didn't stay dead. God resurrected him, and that's what God wants to do for you.

Isn't it time you allowed God to resurrect your life through his love? Isn't it time you allowed God to resurrect your love of yourself by proving to you that you are worthwhile, you are lovable? When John says that God so loved the world, he means God so loved you. God's love is both global and personal.

> My dear children, let's not just talk about love; let's practice real love. This is the only way we'll know we're living truly, living in God's reality. It is also the way to shut down debilitating self-criticism, even when there is something to it. For God is greater than our worried hearts and knows more about us than we do ourselves.
>
> 1 John 3:18–20 MSG

14

Live Face Forward

I hate who I am." Rob stopped and took a deep breath. "I've screwed up so much of my life." Internally, I had to agree. His second marriage was tottering, his kids were barely speaking to him, he was on a cornucopia of medications, and he was stressed out, angry, and intensely unhappy. "Screwed up" was an accurate depiction.

"Okay," I finally said. "What's next?"

"I don't know," he admitted.

"I suggest you find out." I purposely kept any sympathy out of my voice and used an almost confrontational tone. Generally, that's not my approach, but I could sense that Rob expected me to go into the "oh, it's not that bad" routine. The problem was, his life was that bad, and he needed to recognize and accept the reality.

There comes a point in life when the blinders come off, the fog lifts—use whatever analogy you want—and the truth of life smacks you in the face. It can be truth about what's happened to you or others or truth about what you've done to yourself or others. Generally, it's a very painful truth—triumphs don't seem to be as

211

difficult to recognize and experience. When you finally acknowledge the truth, it's normal to stand there, stunned, for a moment. What you do next reveals the sort of person you are. Some people never seem to get over the shock and remain rooted in that moment.

Running Backwards

I started running several years ago. Nothing earth-shattering but enough to keep in shape and get away from my desk, my chair, my phone. Running is a simple thing to do in a complicated world. I like it.

I run face forward. It's easier than running backward. Running face forward allows me to be aware of rocks and curbs and piles of, well, piles. Face forward makes sense in running.

Face forward makes sense in living too. Some men spend their lives living backwards. They may make forward progress, but it is done while their focus and attention are behind them.

Some men live backwards because the view is so horrible, they can't seem to look away. They are like drivers who pass a freeway crash—they find it impossible to take their eyes off the horror. They may be inching ahead in life, but their attention lingers on the crash. Even when they do look forward, that look doesn't last long because they keep whipping their heads around or checking their rearview mirrors. Their eyes may finally orient to the road ahead, but their minds remain fixated behind on the crash.

Charlie was one of those people. The crash was his daughter's disability. From the moment Debbie was born with cerebral palsy, he couldn't take his eyes off the crash. He started living backwards. He wanted to know who was at fault. He wanted to know why her. He wanted to know why him. The answers didn't appear to lie ahead, so Charlie kept searching the past, trying to find something he missed.

To Charlie, the crash of Debbie's condition was a life-altering event—it altered his perception of life, of fairness, of divine justice. And it was a life-ending event—it ended the dream of a life he could no longer have. Every time he looked at Debbie, he couldn't help but wonder what she would look like if she hadn't been born with cerebral palsy. At some point, he began to look away from her altogether, ensuring the major caregiving duties were done by Janet, his wife, and their oldest daughter. Charlie continued to materially provide for Debbie, but he left the emotional care and support to others. He couldn't seem to get over the shock.

Then he found pornography. Pornography was a way to recapture that moment in time before the crash, when he was young and virile and hadn't produced a "defective" child. The women he viewed online didn't have flaws, and a sexual experience with them through masturbation obviously couldn't produce any offspring.

Over time, without realizing it, Charlie came to resent his wife, Janet, subconsciously blaming her for their daughter's disability. As Charlie withdrew from Debbie and left caregiving to Janet, the marriage relationship changed. It became less physical. Janet, tired by the demands of caring for Debbie, didn't seem to object, which Charlie took as tacit approval. Getting his sex online was easier than dealing with the complexity of his relationship with Janet and the complications of Debbie's condition. Pornography became the one activity more compelling than the crash.

Not everyone who lives backward does so because of a tragedy. Some people live backward because they prefer the view. Whatever lies behind appears to be more desirable, more real, more satisfying than anything possible ahead. The highlights and triumphs and bright spots behind continue to capture their gaze. They spend their time reliving the glory, convinced they've already used up their fifteen minutes of fame.

Doug lived life backwards because he preferred the view. Doug was one of those guys who dominated in sports. During his senior year in high school, college scouts would come out and watch him play. Doug was a valuable commodity back then. Multiple schools offered him scholarships, and he went with the best one, to the biggest school. Arriving on campus, Big Doug soon discovered there were larger people in the world and on the field. He still did well in college, but there were no pro scouts watching that senior year, waiting for him to graduate. With football over, Doug felt like a part of his life was over too. That's when life got a little harder and looking back got a little easier.

Gambling was a way of living backwards for Doug. Gambling was cut and dried: you won, you lost. Gambling could be competitive: you won, someone else lost. Gambling reminded Doug of the black-and-white perspective of the gridiron. When he won, it seemed as if the world was back in proper alignment. When he won big, he was noticed. The audience applauded. Strangers came up to congratulate him. Once again, Doug was a valuable commodity.

I understand the value of reconciling with your past. But there has to be more than that. Understanding your past isn't so you can remain fixated on it. Understanding your past isn't merely so you can be reminded of the pain. Instead, understanding your past allows you to accurately assess how you got to where you are now. It is meant to clarify the present. The past is an important place to visit, but you don't want to live there.

What's Next

Generally, I love to watch football, but as a therapist, I find a part of football difficult to watch. It's hard to watch kickers who miss, especially kickers who miss on the final play of the game or at the end of a must-make drive. It doesn't matter if the snap was bad or the kick was long or the angle was off; kickers are expected to make it. When they don't, I get a drop-to-the-bottom jolt in my gut because I know that guy's going to beat himself up for days.

Each of us is an amalgamation of our experiences and the choices we've made because of those experiences. Because we live in a less-than-ideal world, many of those experiences produce pain. Because we are not perfect, many of those choices produce pain. The goal in life should not be to avoid pain—that is not possible. The goal in life should be to use the pain that happens to power something better. The goal in life should be to use that pain to power what's next.

What do you do when you miss the kick? What's next? Too many men spend their lives stuck at the point of the missed kick, and staying stuck isn't the answer. The real answer is to learn everything you can from the missed kick so you're better prepared to make the next one.

Do you remember game 6 of the 2011 World Series between the St. Louis Cardinals and the Texas Rangers? I do, and not only because our division rivals, the Rangers, somehow managed to get into the World Series. I remember that game because there was a "missed kick" moment in the fifth inning. David Freese, the Cardinals' third baseman, was playing in front of a hometown crowd, having grown up in St. Louis. At the start of the fifth inning, Freese inexplicably dropped a routine fly ball hit by the Rangers' Josh Hamilton, who went in to score, putting Texas up by one. I can still see the bobble in my mind. There was absolutely no reason why Freese should have let that ball pop out of his mitt. He missed the "kick" and had no one to blame but himself. The fifth inning of game 6 was a painful one for David Freese. Hometown kid drops a routine pop-up, allowing the dread Josh Hamilton to score and the other team to go ahead and possibly win the Series. So, what's next?

Bottom of the ninth, the Cardinals are down by two runs. David Freese is still in the game and up to bat with two outs. Freese is sitting on two strikes against Ranger closer Naftali Felix when he hits a two-RBI triple and ties the game 7-7. Pandemonium breaks out in St. Louis and in my living room. The game goes into extra innings. In the top of the tenth, Josh Hamilton hits a two-run homer to give Texas the lead. The Cardinals manage to tie it up in the bottom of the tenth, and the game goes into the eleventh inning. With the Rangers scoreless through their at bat, it's time for the Cardinals to be up. Once again, enter David Freese, who goes on to hit only the fourth walk-off home run in a game 6 of a World Series. After this amazing win, the Cardinals go on to take game 7 and the Series. David Freese goes on to be named the 2011 World Series MVP. Game 6 was quite possibly the most exciting game of baseball I've ever watched. One of the best things about that game was the redemption of David Freese.

Staying in the Game

Living backwards doesn't allow you to redeem the past. Redemption can only happen moving forward. I'll bet David Freese hated himself in the fifth inning for missing that pop-up. He stood there stunned for a moment, incredulous at what just happened. How does a major league ballplayer, someone who is paid a great deal of money to catch balls, drop such an easy one? How does that happen? It happens because that's life. Balls get dropped, even by professionals. So, what's next?

Do you think that when David Freese was up to bat in the ninth inning, with two outs and two strikes, he was thinking about that dropped ball? I can almost guarantee it. But I'll bet he wasn't thinking about it to immobilize himself. I'll bet he was thinking about it to motivate himself.

What motivates you when you miss the kick or drop the ball? Are you even motivated to do anything after such an event? David Freese didn't slump in the dugout, eating sunflower seeds and kicking himself for very long. I'm sure he did for a bit, but he was ready to meet the challenge when it came up in the ninth. He stayed in the game.

I don't know what's happened to you or what you've done in response, but I do know you have to stay in the game, no matter what. Charlie needed to accept he'd dropped the ball where his daughter and his wife were concerned. He kept trying to leave the game by escaping to the internet, but he needed to realize that hiding out and lying to himself wasn't helping anyone. Doug needed to accept he'd dropped the ball on making something of his life off the football field, no matter how many times he won at poker. Both of them needed to make a choice to get back in the game.

Build on the Positive

After Rob figured out he dropped the ball in so many areas of his life, he started the difficult process of reconstruction. Though his first marriage ended in divorce, he'd learned a great deal about himself during the process. Together, we worked to quantify those lessons and put them to work saving his second marriage. It was true his kids weren't speaking to him, but most of that had to do with his foul temper and emotional detachment. Rob was surprised by the capacity of his children to forgive his dropped balls and missed kicks where they were concerned and to allow him another chance at bat for their affections. He didn't hit home runs right away, but he didn't strike out completely either. As for his health, Rob needed to understand how a healthy body was necessary to carry out the goals he had in life, now that he was living it again. Recognizing he wasn't young anymore was a hit to his ego, but that recognition is making it easier to adjust his choices to maximize a middle-aged life.

Charlie began by facing the truth of his pornography addiction. He stopped blaming Janet and took responsibility for himself. Once he stopped blaming others, he took back control and made a decision to change how he looked at his daughter, Debbie. Instead of seeing a negative every time he looked at her, he decided to focus on the positives—Debbie's courage, her sweet nature, her tenacity and perseverance through adversity. Instead of seeing a defective child, he realized he was living with an amazingly resilient and exemplary young woman. Charlie came to see that the defect all along was his attitude, not her disability.

Charlie's relationship with Janet was difficult to repair. Janet's resentment over his attitude and choices went deep. She required proof of Charlie's sincerity and only found it after a year of watching his continued commitment to Debbie, to her care both physically and emotionally. Debbie's forgiveness showed Janet the path to her own.

Doug, unfortunately, is still living backwards. He hasn't hit rock bottom yet because, at present, he's winning enough to keep gambling. There will come a point when that's no longer true, but Doug isn't there yet. I see him every once in a while around town, eating at the local coffee shop. He doesn't look up or acknowledge me, and I don't force it. You can't force someone to want to change; they have to understand the reasons and seek change for themselves.

Taking Charge

You've screwed up—admit it. You missed the kick, dropped the ball. What's next? You can continue to beat yourself up or hide from the truth, but there is a better way. Why not take the rubble of your mistakes and use it to build your future? I was listening to the radio the other day and heard someone say the bricks in a dead-end wall can be used to pave the way out. You just have to be willing to do the work to take down the wall and redeem the bricks for something better.

Maybe you're one of those amazingly stubborn men who grab on to an idea or concept and refuse to let go. That brick is called pigheaded. The capacity for stubbornness, though, doesn't have to be negative when it's used for something positive. A stubborn person could also be called tenacious, determined, firm, or steadfast. How can you rework your stubbornness, turning it from a negative into a positive?

Maybe you're one of those laser-focused men who has an ability to disregard everything around you. That brick could be marked self-absorption, or it could be called concentration; it depends what you're focusing on. If you've been focusing strictly on yourself, your needs, wants, and desires, how could you broaden out that focus and include the betterment of other people?

Maybe you're one of those anything-goes kind of guys who laughs and jokes and skates through life without really taking responsibility for anything. That brick could be called undependable, but it doesn't need to be completely discarded. The ability to laugh at one's self, to refuse to take life too seriously, is a valuable paver on difficult roads. How can you smooth off the edges and reshape that careless, negative attitude into a carefree, positive one?

Maybe you're one of those men who has hidden out all your life, refusing to fully engage in life by living quietly behind the scenes. That

219

brick could be called timidity, and you might be tempted to discard it. However, with a few extra layers, that timid core could provide the foundation for a perceptive understanding and affinity toward the forgotten, the downtrodden, and the oppressed. How can you use your own sense of marginalization to create a boldness to help others?

Maybe you're one of those men who believes that nothing is right unless everything is. This brick is called perfectionism and can exist as the capstone to many dead-end walls. Perfectionism is a very tough stone but when broken can still provide solidity of purpose and the strength of excellence. How can you break through your perfectionism and still use parts of that rigidity for structure and support?

I used a wall analogy before, but this time I want you to take a piece of paper, which will represent the dead-end wall your choices have produced. Next, fold the paper into sections. Each section constitutes a "brick." Label as many bricks as you can with the negative things about yourself that have caused you to miss the kick, to drop the ball.

Cut out your bricks. This is you breaking down your wall. With your bricks in front of you, for every one that you can, come up with something positive or potentially positive about that personality trait or event or negative characteristic. Try to find something positive to redeem every one, even if it is only to provide you with motivation never to have such a thing happen to you or by you again.

As you come up with your positives, lay out your bricks in a straight line, moving forward, away from yourself.

It's not possible to remake the past; it is what it is. The true possibility lies in using the past, whatever it is, to intentionally use the material of that past to build a better future. A few men will be so far gone, so evil, that the thought of doing this simply does not enter their minds. Most men truly want to be better, to do better, to find a way to the ninth and eleventh inning after the disastrous fifth. Most men want redemption in their lives, with their families, with themselves. They already have what it takes to reach redemption. All they need is help to find the way.

Reaching Higher

Too many men live in a backwards woulda-coulda-shoulda world. Again, as a therapist, I understand the necessity of figuring out your past—but the reason is so you can get on with the present and build a better future. When you start to believe in yourself, in God, and in his ability to love you, goals become possible again.

God does not want you to live stuck in your past. He wants to make a difference in your life today. He has a future waiting for you that he wants you to experience and enjoy. The apostle Paul put it this way:

> Friends, don't get me wrong: By no means do I count myself an expert in all of this, but I've got my eye on the goal, where God is beckoning us onward—to Jesus. I'm off and running, and I'm not turning back.
>
> Philippians 3:13–14 MSG

Woulda-coulda-shoulda forces you to keep circling around. You need to live life off and running, toward the goal. I'm not saying this race is going to be a sprint and that you won't have some tough hills to climb—because you will. But you'll never finish if you don't run forward. You'll never finish if you bow out of the race.

There are so many substitutes you can use for the real race. They appear invigorating, muscular, and competitive, but it's like suiting up at a track meet and running sprints on the sidelines but never getting out on the field. Being at a track meet is not the same as running in a race. This life is a challenging race with a proud Father cheering you on every step of the way.

15

Ask For and Accept Help

Are you kidding?" he said. "Nobody knows I'm here." Even though I'd asked, I already knew the answer. Most men want to keep counseling quiet—some men appear more willing to admit to erectile dysfunction than admit to going to counseling, as if the latter was somehow more emasculating than the former. I suspected Tyler fell into that category.

"Your wife knows you're here," I pointed out.

"Well, yeah, but I meant other people. I'm not going to broadcast I'm in counseling." He said *counseling* like it was a dirty word. I chose to overlook the dig to my chosen profession.

"Fair enough," I responded. "It's fine to keep your counseling private. That's up to you. But have you shared with anyone besides your wife what you've been working on here?"

"No, not really. I've been keeping this private," he said with a look that communicated "Why wouldn't I?"

"It's not a bad idea to bounce ideas off other people," I suggested. "You wouldn't have to say you're in counseling if you don't want to. Have you thought of getting together with at least one other guy to go over some of this stuff?"

"I'm getting together with you," Tyler said flatly, as if stating the obvious.

"That's right, and we're doing good work," I assured him. "I just thought you might benefit from opening up a little bit with one or two other guys. Someone you trust. Someone who could support the work you're doing with me."

Tyler looked puzzled. "I've never really given it any thought. I don't even know who I'd ask." He looked unsettled, although I wasn't sure if it was because he couldn't think of anyone or he wasn't comfortable with the whole idea.

Men can have difficulty working down to deeper levels of conversation with other men. Women seem much more willing to dive into those waters with each other. It's not surprising, really, given that women can be much more comfortable verbally and emotionally than men. I've observed this to be both a blessing and a curse in my own practice.

Sometimes, women give out their feelings so freely it's as if they place little or no value on them. I've seen women verbally vomit the emotional contents of their thoughts without considering the consequences to others, especially in group settings. Devastating pronouncements can sometimes be made with startling ease.

Men, on the other hand, are often slow to reveal what they're really thinking. It's as if these thoughts, feelings, and emotions need more time and energy to break through the surface. Often, these eruptions are predicated by smaller, sarcastic, under-the-breath observations or comments. When a man finally opens up, it could release years of silence, not just days or months. Sometimes, the final latch to be unlocked to openness comes through finding a kindred spirit, another man who's gone through something similar and who understands.

Companions

When we were younger, we had friends, good friends, we could tell our thoughts to. We may have done it while playing games or walking to school or riding bikes. Most men I've talked to about this can immediately name their childhood buddy, first and last name, tell me what he looked like and the last time they were together. Interestingly, many of those men are no longer in contact with that friend. Time and distance has created a separation, and that friend has never been replaced. If a man is married, he'll have his spouse to confide in, as he should, but it is a loss when a man does not have a deeply personal male friendship.

Adult men have trouble putting down the horns and taking off the masks in order to cultivate friendship. As I said before, this is a loss because only true friendship allows men to develop the important male component of accountability. Each of us needs other guys who will call us on our stuff, tell us to knock it off, and *thwap* us upside the head when we're veering off down the lane of utter stupidity. This kind of companionship is rare and unbelievably necessary in this world we live in.

It used to be men stayed within the context of family. They had grandfathers and dads, uncles and brothers and cousins to watch and observe as far as manhood was concerned. The family had universal permission to comment and criticize and, yes, counsel on what they were doing, how they were doing, why they were doing, and with whom they were doing. There was accountability within the family.

It used to be men stayed within the context of location. They didn't move around every few years, and boys grew up to be men while that maturation was overseen by every other mom and dad and adult authority figure in town. It was hard to get away with anything when everyone was watching. There was accountability within the proverbial village.

It used to be men stayed within the context of profession. They chose a profession, or one was chosen for them, and they became an apprentice to an older, more skilled man. They learned their trade from him and the other guys, but they also learned about life and about being a man from at least one other guy along the way. There was accountability within the profession or the trade.

In all of these situations, a man was part of a larger context. Yes, he was considered an adult man in his own right, but his manhood was not divorced from these other contexts of family, of location, of profession. Accountability tended to keep him in line, provided him with examples to follow and mentors to assist. If he had a problem, he had a variety of places he could go to for help. Too many men have nowhere else to go and no one to ask for help, unless they happen to find me or someone like me. This isolation creates a deep sense of loss and vulnerability, making it that much more attractive to hide out and run away from the pain.

Band of Brothers

I'm not much for graphic video games. Perhaps if they had come into vogue when I was younger, I'd be able to connect with them. As it is, I barely have enough time to brush my teeth in the morning, let alone spend hours fighting aliens or carjacking Mustangs. That isn't to say, however, that I don't understand the immense draw these games have for the male gender. They are exciting and visual. They allow for acceptable expressions of aggression and provide opportunities for competition in a world of participation trophies.

So many of these games are based on warfare. More than that, they allow for you to be part of a team, a unit, a group of fellow soldiers banded together in common purpose. The graphics are gritty and the violence disturbingly real, even when it involves alien enemies and landscapes. They are compelling on a variety of levels, including their ability to re-create a sense of joint mission and purpose with even a simulated band of brothers.

I'm reminded of the quintessential war movie, *Saving Private Ryan*. The opening scenes of violence, depicting the events of the Allied invasion of Normandy, remain with me to this day. Another aspect of the movie that continues to stay with me is the sense of unity and purpose portrayed by the group of soldiers assigned to, as the movie says, save Private Ryan. If you haven't watched the movie, I encourage you to, but be warned, it's emotionally powerful. Separated from family, from location, and from profession, this small group of men creates a different sort of family in the midst of war. I think one of the reasons this movie was so wildly successful is because of this very depiction and confirmation that unity and camaraderie and brotherhood are possible even in devastating circumstances.

I don't know what sort of circumstances you're facing. I don't know what sort of enemies you're looking in the eye. I don't know what's waiting for you over the next ridge. But, whatever it is, I do know you'll be stronger and better off with a group of guys to support you than you would be alone.

By a group of guys, I don't just mean any guys. I don't mean guys who are so caught up in their own stuff that they can't watch your back. I don't mean guys who are more interested in what you do than in who you are. And I don't necessarily mean guys who look exactly like you.

When looking for a band of brothers, you need to choose guys who have enough of their own stuff together that they're able to be outward focused. If you're fighting a pornography addiction, you don't want to choose someone who's in the midst of the same thing himself. If you're trying to stay sober, you don't want to choose someone who refuses to admit to his own drinking problem. If you're trying to restrain from a sexual addiction, you don't want to choose someone who envies your lifestyle. Instead, you want to choose someone who has strength of character and is farther down the road to recovery than you. Otherwise, that person may drag you down.

When looking for a band of brothers, you need to choose guys who want to be with you. There are lots of venues for guys to get together. It is an error, however, to think that guys show up because of you instead of the activity. Some guys just want to play baseball or soccer. To them, you're a position on the field, not really a person. These guys won't be interested in getting to know you better, because that will take time away from whatever the activity is. You're a glorified sparring partner or a punching bag or an opposing jersey. Instead, watch for guys who stop that extra minute to ask you how you are, who appear interested in your life, and who actually tell you the truth when you ask how they're doing.

You also want to watch out for the opposite. These are the guys who are only involved in the activity as a way to get to you. These guys aren't necessarily looking for you in particular, just someone like you. They are looking for business contacts, someone to loan them money, a couch to sleep on. They can be very easygoing guys, but their focus is decidedly inward. They'll listen to what you have to say, all the while figuring out how to get what they want. These guys are grown-up adolescents, grown-up drinking and smoking buddies.

When looking for a band of brothers, consider those who look different from you. Don't rule out different ethnicities and age groups. We tend to choose people who look like us if we're not intentional about expanding our horizons. The person who connects with us the best may be someone who on the outside appears to be quite different. Life sometimes throws such serendipitous curveballs our way.

Finally, as you're bringing together your band of brothers, remember that you're one of the brothers too. Don't be afraid to include someone who could benefit from you, your experiences, and even your struggles. The best camaraderie happens with mutual benefit. Give-and-take is healthy, and sometimes the best way to get over your own struggle is to help someone else with theirs.

Taking Charge

You may be one of those guys who already has a strong connection to other guys through family or location or profession. If so, I congratulate you and suggest you deepen those bands even more by sharing the struggles and the truths you've uncovered while reading this book. You may even want to go through it again with someone else. It's certainly designed to be able to do that, in a group of two or larger.

You may be one of those guys who is isolated from the type of friendships necessary to really feel comfortable sharing your struggles and challenges. You can still go through this book by yourself (obviously, you have). However, in this last chapter, I encourage you to think about who you know that might become the first in your band of brothers. It could be someone you knew in the past but haven't taken the time to make contact with. In this internet age, your band of brothers doesn't all have to be in the same place. Ideally, at least one other person should be geographic, but don't let location stop you from exploring a connection. Here are some suggestions:

- When deciding who might be open to a deeper friendship, don't forget to factor in what you bring to the table. Friendships are mutual with reciprocity.
- Choose someone you admire, who displays masculine attributes you value.
- Keep trying. You're not going to bat a thousand in your search. Some people simply won't be interested and you'll need to move on.
- Allow the relationship to deepen naturally. Don't try to force it.
- Be patient but not too patient. If it's taking weeks between conversations or activities, you may want to move on to someone else.
- If you're dealing with a specific issue, like pornography or sexual addiction or overeating or substance abuse or gambling, there are support groups in the community you can take advantage of, as a way to provide broader support as you're working on finding and cultivating closer friendships.

Sometimes this life can be a real battle. Circumstances may have separated you from the natural male accountability and camaraderie of family, location, or profession, but you can still expend the effort to draw a small group of men around you. Having them with you in battle may just allow you to win the war.

Reaching Higher

Jesus had his own band of brothers, also known as the disciples (Matt. 10:1–3). After he left, these men stuck together, faced astonishing adversity, and altered the course of history. I'm not suggesting you need to accomplish something similar, but even Jesus thought it was a good idea to walk through life with a group of guys. If Jesus didn't do this life solo, why should you?

Solomon, the writer of Ecclesiastes, said:

> By yourself you're unprotected. With a friend you can face the worst. Can you round up a third? A three-stranded rope isn't easily snapped.
>
> Ecclesiastes 4:12 MSG

As you're rounding up that third, I'd like you to remember another time-honored piece of wisdom—the Golden Rule: do unto others as you would have them do unto you. In other words, as you're looking for the type of friends who can make a difference in your life, start first by being that type of friend yourself. The more you emulate the qualities of friendship, the more you will draw like-minded people to you. You're not the only guy out there looking for a good friend.

All of this means, of course, that you'll need to stop isolating, you'll need to stop numbing, you'll need to stop engaging in your compulsive behaviors. In order to cultivate friendship, you'll need to devote a significant portion of time to the effort. When you do, you may find that real-life friendship is more compelling than anything you could do in secret or online.

It is my prayer that you will continue to grow and develop into the man God created you to be. He has big plans for you; I know. Allow me to quote just one more verse. It's the theme verse for the work we do at my facility, The Center for Counseling and Health Resources:

> "For I know the plans I have for you," declares the LORD, "plans to prosper you and not to harm you. Plans to give you hope and a future."
>
> Jeremiah 29:11

I see this verse lived out in the lives of men every day. May this verse and this promise become your all-consuming reality today and in the future.

Notes

1. blog.cytalk.com/2010/01/web-porn-revenue/.

2. http://www.brainyquote.com/quotes/quotes/t/tacitus118925.html, accessed August 11, 2011.

3. http://www.azcentral.com/news/articles/2011/08/24/20110824wallow-fire-cousins-charged.html.

4. http://usscouts.org/usscouts/advance/boyscout/bslaw.asp.

5. Jerry Pawloski, "Father-Daughter Renaissance 'Fight' Ends in Arrests," *The Olympian*, October 18, 2011.

6. http://pubs.niaaa.nih.gov/publications/arh28-2/78-79.htm.

7. "The Madoff Scheme: Meet the Liquidator," *CBS News*, June 20, 2010, http://www.cbsnews.com/stories/2009/09/24/60minutes/main5339719.shtml?tag=currentVideoInfo;segmentUtilities.

8. http://www.brainyquote.com/quotes/quotes/p/philmcgraw177364.html.

Gregory L. Jantz, PhD, is a popular speaker and award-winning author of more than 25 books, including *Healing the Scars of Emotional Abuse* and *Every Woman's Guide to Managing Your Anger*. He is the founder of The Center for Counseling & Health Resources, Inc. (www.aplaceofhope.com) in the state of Washington. Information about Dr. Jantz can be found at drgregoryjantz.com.

Ann McMurray has coauthored several books, including *Healing the Scars of Emotional Abuse* and *Every Woman's Guide to Managing Your Anger*. She too lives in Washington and works at The Center for Counseling & Health Resources, Inc.

YOU CAN LIVE FREE FROM ANXIETY

OVERCOMING
ANXIETY, WORRY, AND FEAR

Practical Ways to Find Peace

GREGORY L. JANTZ, PhD

WITH ANN McMURRAY

With compassion, common sense, and biblical wisdom, Dr. Jantz will help you identify the causes of your anxiety, assess the severity of your symptoms, and start down avenues for positive change.

Revell
a division of Baker Publishing Group
www.RevellBooks.com

Available Wherever Books Are Sold
Also Available in Ebook Format

HOPE AND HEALING FOR THE VICTIMS OF EMOTIONAL ABUSE

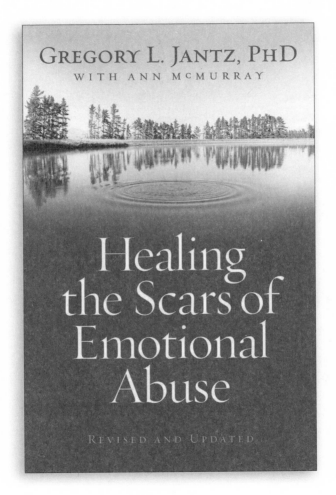

Revell
a division of Baker Publishing Group
www.RevellBooks.com

Available Wherever Books Are Sold

Be the First to Hear about Other New Books from Revell!

Sign up for announcements about new and upcoming titles at

www.revellbooks.com/signup

Follow us on twitter
RevellBooks

Join us on facebook
Revell

Don't miss out on our great reads!

Revell
a division of Baker Publishing Group
www.RevellBooks.com